Translated Texts for Historians

This series is designed to meet the needs of students of ancient and medieval history and others who wish to broaden their study by reading source material, but whose knowledge of Latin or Greek is not sufficient to allow them to do so in the original language. Many important Late Imperial and Dark Age texts are currently unavailable in translation and it is hoped that TTH will help to fill this gap and to complement the secondary literature in English which already exists. The series relates principally to the period 300–800 AD and includes Late Imperial, Greek, Byzantine and Syriac texts as well as source books illustrating a particular period or theme. Each volume is a self-contained scholarly translation with an introductory essay on the text and its author and notes on the text indicating major problems of interpretation, including textual difficulties.

Cover illustration: Vandal jewellery found near Hippo Regius, N. Africa

Translated Texts for Historians
Volume 10

Victor of Vita:
History of the
Vandal Persecution

Translated with notes and introduction by
JOHN MOORHEAD

Liverpool
University
Press

First published 1992 by
Liverpool University Press
PO Box 147, Liverpool, L69 3BX

British Library Cataloguing-in-Publication Data
A British Library CIP Record is available
ISBN 0 85323 127 3

Printed in Great Britain at
The Alden Press in the City of Oxford

CONTENTS

Contents

ACKNOWLEDGEMENTS

It is a pleasure to thank those people who have helped in the preparation of this short book. The Department of History at the University of Queensland enabled me to spend a period in London working on a draft, which benefited greatly from the comments of the publisher's reader. Serena Bagley and Mary Kooyman presided over the production of the final manuscript with a high degree of both efficiency and tact, while Liverpool University Press and those associated with Translated Texts for Historians have always been helpful. Finally, I should record that my parents, John and Pauline, were present during a time of intensive work on the text, and that from their astonished reactions to Victor's narrative, as in many other things, I have continued to learn from them.

John Moorhead
Feast of the Transfiguration, 1991

INTRODUCTION

Among those peoples who occupied the territory of the Roman empire in the West in the fifth century and who, in accordance with the perspective of the Romans, are conventionally termed 'barbarians', the Vandals occupy an important place.[1] Having crossed the Rhine in the company of other tribal groups on New Year's Eve 406 they intermittently moved south-west through Gaul and Spain until 429, when, shortly after the accession of king Geiseric (428-477), they crossed the straits of Gibraltar and moved into Roman Africa. It was a desirable territory: a writer of the mid-fourth century had described Africa as 'rich in all things. It is adorned with all goods, grains as well as beasts, and almost alone it supplies to all peoples the oil they need.'[2] Indeed, the export of oil may account for the remains of African pottery of late antiquity which, as recent archaeological work is revealing, achieved a 'worldwide' distribution, a phenomenon which is currently suggesting major reinterpretations of the economic history of late antiquity.[3] The Vandals made good headway, and in 435 Geiseric concluded a treaty with the Empire which granted them a considerable portion of the land of Africa, based on Numidia. But in 439 he made a surprise move eastward into proconsular Africa and occupied Carthage, the capital of Roman Africa. An expeditionary force sent against the Vandals failed to reach its destination, and in the following year a second treaty awarded them the proconsular province, Byzacena, Tripolitania and part of Numidia. The remaining, western part of Africa remained in the hands of the Romans, and so the Vandals were confirmed in their possession of the richest areas. From there they launched expeditions against many parts of the

---

[1] Incomparably the most important work is that of Courtois 1955, whose status as the standard synthesis is secure for the foreseeable future. Nevertheless it must be said that in both this work and his shorter study on Victor 1954 the tone he adopts towards this author is hypercritical; see Chatillon 1955 and Marrou 1967. Courtois has also come under attack for the sharpness of the distinction he draws between civilized and 'forgotten' Africa: Whittaker 1978. Prosopography is now on a more secure footing, thanks to the works of Maier 1973, Martindale 1980 and Mandouze 1982; note as well the comments of Diesner 1968. Archaeology is yielding more results, as shown by the work of Koenig 1981.

[2] *Expositio totius mundi et gentium* 61. Note that the Visigoth Alaric was presumably leading his people towards Africa when he died at Consentia in Bruttium in 410 (literary sources listed in *PLRE* 2: 48).

[3] Carandini 1983, and more generally Giardina 1986.

Mediterranean, and in 455 Geiseric was able to take advantage of instability in Rome to attack the city. In 460 the emperor Majorian sent a fleet against the Vandals, but nothing came of the expedition; in 468 the emperor Leo launched an attack on an astonishing scale, but it too failed.[4] The reigns of Geiseric's eldest son Huneric (477-484) and the subsequent kings show few signs of an aggressive foreign policy, which may possibly be accounted for by troubles the Vandals were experiencing from the African Moors and the need for a greater concentration on internal affairs. Their kingdom did not long outlast the accession of the emperor Justinian in 527: in 533 he sent against it his general Belisarius who defeated the Vandals in a short war, whereupon Africa became a part of the Empire again.

Such events constitute an indispensable background to the work here translated. But only rarely do they intrude on it, for, as the titles affixed to manuscript copies of the work imply, its author, Victor of Vita, was essentially concerned to recount the Vandals' persecution of the Catholics of Africa, from the time of their arrival in 429 until 484, in which year he seems to have written virtually all his work. This concern governed Victor's selection of material, and if his opening chapters are sometimes couched in vague language and problematic in their chronology, he proceeds to give a minutely detailed account of numerous atrocities inflicted on the Catholics in the proconsular province. Compared to the benignly tolerant Ostrogoths in Italy, or the intermittently persecuting Visigoths in Gaul and Spain, other Arian peoples who settled in Roman territory and are similarly known from accounts written by Catholics, the Vandals emerge from Victor's account as thoroughly nasty. Doubtless other emphases were possible in describing them; the moralist Salvian, for example, writing not long after the arrival of the Vandals, expressed pleasure that the Vandals cleaned up the lax sexual practices which had been rife in Africa.[5] Victor was aware that not everyone shared his outlook (cf below 3.62), and recent work is making clear continuities between Roman and Vandal Africa: for example, we know of the continued existence of

---

[4] It has been calculated that the sum expended on the campaign was at least six times that spent by Justinian on the construction of Hagia Sophia: Courtois 1955: 201.

[5] *Gub dei* 7.22 in particular, but cf. 7.14 for the author's concern with this theme. Salvian is cited as representing a point of view; there is no need to take him seriously as evidence.

provinces for administrative purposes, while developments in urban evolution in the Vandal period can be seen as part of long-term trends, and the export of pottery continued, if on a reduced level.[6] But, assuming that some degree of reality underlies Victor's tale of woe, we may ask why the Vandals behaved in a way which allows them to be seen as more ferocious than their Gothic co-religionists.

The earlier part of Victor's narrative, which deals with the activities of the Vandals before and after the capture of Carthage, suggests that at this stage their behaviour was motivated chiefly by a desire to gain control of the wealth of the indigenous people who were, as it happened, Catholics. That such behaviour created more animosity than that of the Goths is not to be wondered at, for, although the precise mechanism whereby the Goths were given access to the wealth of the territories they took over remains the subject of debate, it is clear that this was in accordance with an orderly system which, in Italy at any rate, was put in place by a Roman, the praetorian prefect Liberius.[7] This was certainly not the case with the Vandals, who helped themselves. Bishops and clergy were indeed to the fore among the victims of Geiseric's wrath, but this answered to the wealth of their churches; on one occasion the king demanded a change in the religious allegiance of Sebastian, but this was merely a pretext for doing away with him for political reasons (Victor 1.19).[8] Nevertheless, if Geiseric's persecution of Catholics was motivated by economic considerations one would have expected it to have lessened as the Vandals increasingly gained control of their wealth. Yet the reverse happened, and from the period beginning with the death of bishop Deogratias, which occurred before the end of 457 (Victor 1.27), persecution based on religion predominates. Only then does Victor explicitly mention that the Vandals were Arians (persistently spelt by him 'Arrians'), referring to their allegiance to the doctrine of Arius, a heretic of the early fourth century who, contrary to the Catholics, referred to by the Vandals as 'homousians', emphasised the degree of difference between the Father

---

[6]   Continued existence of provinces: Chastagnol 1967. Urban evolution: Thébert 1983. Pottery: Carandini 1983:151. Continuity in other spheres is explored by Clover 1982b, 1986.

[7]   Goffart 1980 provides a challenging revisionist account.

[8]   cf. the 'heuristic principle' enunciated by Diesner 1962: 108f.

and the Son and denied that they were of one substance; only then (1.30 onwards) does Victor begin to employ such words as 'martyrdom' and 'confessor.' The death of Geiseric in 477 seems to have brought some relief to the persecuted, but under his successor Huneric (spelt 'Huniric' by Victor and 'Hunirix' in official documents he reproduces) conditions soon worsened, and it became clear that religion was now the point at issue. As far as the Byzantine author Procopius was aware, persecution of a specifically religious kind only began with Huneric, and given that he had arrived in Africa with the army of Belisarius he was in a position to have access to local traditions.[9] Finally, in 484 an edict was issued which sought to impose Arianism on the Catholics, and in the succeeding months persecution reached its peak.[10] We may therefore accept Victor's assertion that there were two reasons for the persecution: 'the loss of souls and the plunder of property' (3.63). Both religious and economic factors were involved.

Victor's narrative, then, can be read as a document describing a particularly bad case of relations between Romans and occupying barbarians, and for this reason it constitutes an important record of the period of the *Völkerwanderung*. But this is not the only way in which the text can be approached. A number of modern writers, often arguing from passages in the fifth century authors Orosius (*adv pag* 7.41.7) and Salvian (*gub dei* 7.16.71; see too 5.8), and reports in the letters of Augustine of Hippo of attempts by Arians and schismatic Donatists to make allies of each other (*ep* 44.3.6, 185.1.1), have suggested that the Vandals, as they invaded Africa, enjoyed the support of many Africans who were, for various reasons, unhappy with Roman government.[11] But against this theory it may be argued, firstly, that we should be wary of building upon two rhetorical passages in Orosius and Salvian and from passages of Augustine which were written before the situation they are used to explain came into being, and secondly, that with the

---

[9] *BV* 1.8.3. I doubt whether any anti-catholic sentiment is to be read into Geiseric's famous observation, reported by Procopius, that he was sailing against 'those with whom God is angry' (*BV* 1.5.24).

[10] A different understanding in Frend 1982: 627.

[11] See, with varying degrees of emphasis, Stein 1959: 320f, 327; Diligensky 1961: 246-48; Diesner 1966: 51f; and perhaps Frend 1971: 300. I cannot accept Possidius *V Aug* 23 as evidence that 'the clergy were hated because of their possessions' (so Frend, in Frage 1978:479 n.2).

possible exception of a portion at the end of Victor's work almost certainly not written by him (3.71), we have absolutely no evidence for the Donatists having supported the Vandals. Indeed, one recension of a work of Donatist provenance composed in Vandal Africa demonstrates that the letters in the name 'Gensericus' have the numerical value 666.[12] Nevertheless, the intuition that events which occurred during the Vandal domination of Africa need to be understood in the light of preceding African history, particularly religious history, is entirely sound, and it will be worth our while going into this subject in a little more detail.

Even while the Roman empire was still pagan, African Christianity had displayed distinctive characteristics. It was immensely productive of martyrs, of whom Perpetua and Felicitas in the time of Septimius Severus and bishop Cyprian of Carthage in the time of Valerian are probably the best known, and both literary and archaeological evidence indicate the popularity of the cult of the African martyrs. Africa was also productive of movements resistant to ecclesiastical authority; one thinks of the career of Tertullian and of the confessors whose treatment of the lapsed caused so much trouble for Cyprian. The conversion of the emperor Constantine to Christianity occurred at almost the same time as the outbreak of a major schism in the African church, that of the Donatists. This originated in disagreement as to the attitude to be taken to those who had handed over the scriptures in time of persecution (*traditores*) and those ordained by them, and the defiance of the state practised by the Donatists early in the fifth century was to lead Augustine to develop a theory of coercion which some of his most enthusiastic modern admirers have found distasteful. The independent nature of African Christianity was again demonstrated after the Byzantine reconquest: African theologians, notably bishop Facundus of Hermiane, were to the fore in resisting the condemnation of the Three Chapters which Justinian foisted on the church, even after it had been approved by pope Vigilius and the Council of Constantinople (553), and the seventh

---

[12] *Liber genealogus* F618, *MGH AA* 9: 195. One would like to know more about this text.

century saw the Africans challenge another imperially supported dogma, that of Monothelitism.[13]

These events have no direct connection with the Vandals, but provide a necessary background to the work of Victor of Vita. For an author whose characters are prone to cry out, in words going back to the first generations of Christians, 'Christiani sumus!' (Victor 2.28, 3.17, cf. 3.49), who describes implements of torture which were the same as those used against Christians in the days of the persecutions (below 3.28 with note 13) and *martyres* and *confessores* who pass through *passiones* (2.33) to their *coronae* (1.50, 2.30, 2.34), and who reports an attempt by agents of the state to force clergy to hand over (*tradere*) cultic instruments and books (1.39), is obviously describing a situation which he sees in terms of the great persecutions. Similarly, Victor is almost obsessed with the evil of the rebaptism which the Arians insisted that converts to their persuasion underwent, an issue which seems to rank in his mind as being of roughly equal importance to the Trinity among the issues dividing Catholics from Arians. The anti-Arian arguments of the *Book of the catholic faith*, a work which the catholic bishops prepared for the council summoned by Huneric in 484 and which Victor reproduces (2.56-2.101), are entirely concerned with belief in the Trinity, whereas Victor's stress on rebaptism, on the other hand, reveals concern with an issue which had been a concern of the African church in the time of Cyprian and had called forth polemical writings from Augustine of Hippo against the Donatists.[14] And surely the *Book of the catholic faith* not only recalls the intrepidity and theological acumen of the African bishops who badgered the emperor Honorius concerning the heresy of Pelagius early in the fourth century, but also anticipates the feisty opposition their successors were to display towards the ecclesiastical policies of later Byzantine emperors. Seen in this way, Victor's *History* becomes a document revelatory of not only the barbarian invasions, but of the nature of African Christianity as well. And it suggests that the nature of the memorable encounter between the catholic Christians of Africa and the Vandals owed something to

---

[13] It would be good to have a reliable one volume account; see, perhaps, Cuoq 1984. At a very different level are the excellent comments of Markus 1972 and Cameron 1982.

[14] But note that the Catholics in Victor were forcibly rebaptized and hence compelled to apostatize, so that the grounds underlying the issue were quite different.

the combative traditions of the former as well as the nefarious nature of the latter.

We know little of the author of the work here translated, although the density of scriptural allusions, particularly in the impassioned concluding sections, surely enable a clerical author to be postulated. Various deductions can be made from passages which are written in the first person and the attribution supplied in manuscripts of the *History*, 'sancto victore episcopo patriae vitensi', which is generally accepted to mean 'the holy Victor, a bishop, whose place of origin was Vita.'[15] As it happens, at the time of the council summoned by Huneric in 484 a bishop named Victor governed the see of Vita in Byzacena, and one is naturally tempted to identify this person with the author of the *History*. But the bishop of Vita did not attend the council,[16] whereas it is clear from the narrative in the *History* that its author was among those present. Moreover, his descriptions of his own activities sometimes imply that he was a priest, as when for example he celebrates the divine mysteries (2.28), but never that he was a bishop, and his sustained use of the first person implies that he spent a good deal of time at Carthage; indeed, his ability to reproduce official documents implies that he had access to the archives of the see of Carthage.[17] Nevertheless, Victor does not seem to have been one of the 4966 clergy who were exiled by Huneric, despite his having accompanied them, for he describes himself as being among those who were able to visit them when they were held in confinement (Victor 2.28, 2.32). We may therefore believe that at the time when he wrote his history he was a priest in Carthage, perhaps not formally one of the clergy of the city, who later became a bishop, possibly of Vita, his place of origin.

---

[15] The scanty evidence is discussed by Courtois 1954: 5-10, Pastorino 1980: 48-53, Costanza 1980: 231-39 and 1981: 8-12, and, more briefly, Mandouze 1982: 1175f (Victor 64).

[16] 'non occurrit' is recorded against his name, no. 44 in the list of bishops of Byzacena in the *Notitia provinciarum civitatum Africae* attached to Victor's *Historia* ed. Halm p. 65, ed. Petschenig p. 125. The town of Vita seems otherwise unknown.

[17] He reproduces various edicts of Huneric (2.3f, 2.39, 3.3-14) and a reply to one of these by bishop Eugenius (2.41f), as well as the *Book of the catholic faith*. Pastorino describes Carthage as the epicentre of Victor's story (1980: 77).

It is hard to establish when Victor wrote his work.[18] The opening words may seem to supply a straightforward solution to this question: 'It is evident that this is now the sixtieth year since that cruel and savage people of the Vandal race set foot on the territory of wretched Africa.' As the Vandal invasion of Africa began in May 429,[19] assuming that Victor reckons the years inclusively this would seem to yield a date of 488/489 for the composition of his work. Yet the greater part of the narrative deals with the events of 484: we are told of the meeting called by Huneric which was held in the February of that year, an edict issued by the king on 25 February is reproduced, various atrocities subsequently committed by the Vandals are described, one of which is known from another work, possibly also written by Victor, to have occurred on 2 July,[20] while another is known to have occurred on 24 September,[21] and the narrative concludes with the description of a terrible famine which occurred during one summer, presumably that of 484. The last chapter in the text which has been transmitted to us, which mentions the death of Huneric in December 484, is almost certainly a later addition to the text, for 3.70 can be seen as the conclusion of a rhetorical passage which begins at 3.64, and the effect of 3.71 is sheer bathos.[22] The flow of the narrative therefore suggests 484 as the date of composition, and the circumstance that the exiled bishop Eugenius had already been recalled by the third year of the reign of Huneric's successor[23] could be held to suggest that Victor wrote before that time.

Why, then, does Victor claim to be writing in the sixtieth year from the coming of the Vandals to Africa? Perhaps he reckoned the

---

[18] General discussions: Courtois 1954: 16-22; Pastorino 1980: 53-57; Costanza 1980: 239-45 and 1981: 12-14.

[19] Hydatius *chron* 90, *MGH AA* 11: 21; see Courtois 1955: 155n.2.

[20] Victor 3.41; the date is known from the full title of the *Passio beatissimorum martyrum* which occurs together with the *Historia* in all manuscripts and is printed by Halm and Petschenig immediately following it. That Victor wrote it has been denied by Courtois 1954: 26f. and Pastorino 1980: 61f, but against this Pitkäranta 1974 points out similarities of style.

[21] The burning of Laetus (Victor 2.52) can be dated from Victor of Tunnunna *chron. s.a.* 479.

[22] I am not persuaded by Roncoroni 1977, and Pastorino 1980: 57-61 is more open minded than I would care to be; see, rather, Courtois 1954: 16.

[23] *Laterculus regum VVandalorum et Alanorum* 8 (*MGH AA* 13: 459)

years from a Vandal incursion shortly prior to 429,[24] perhaps he was misinformed as to the date of the arrival of the Vandals in Africa, or perhaps a scribal error distorted what he originally wrote. But there are a few brief passages which must have been written subsequent to the death of Huneric: the hand which wrote 'quod non contingit' at 2.12 was aware that Huneric was not succeeded by his sons, the author of the words 'quod breve fuerat et caducum' at 2.17 knew that Huneric's reign was short and transitory, and another passage which may have been written after 484 occurs in 3.30, where the writer mentions that a victim of the persecution was to be seen in Constantinople. Perhaps Victor lightly revised the manuscript of a work he had written some years earlier before he published it in 488/489, or perhaps someone else added a few touches. In any case, there is no reason to doubt that the text originated in the church of Carthage at a time very close indeed to the events it describes in book three, and that for the most part its perspective is that of an author writing somewhat late in the year 484, with the immediacy but possible lack of perspective that this implies.

The circumstances of the composition of the book raise the difficult question of the purpose for which Victor wrote his history. The only substantial discussion of this question is that provided by Courtois, who argues that Victor's work constitutes a plea for aid from Byzantium written at the behest of bishop Eugenius of Carthage, whose name suggests that he came from the East.[25] Given the linguistic situation which prevailed in Constantinople in the late fifth century it would not have been unreasonable for the author of a work seeking to influence opinion there to have written in Latin, and it is true that the conclusion to Victor's work refers to the African church as having sought help from the East, although I take Victor to have written 'fathers (*patribus*) of the East' rather than 'parts (*partibus*) of the East' (3.68), and would note that the words which follow imply that a plea had already been made unsuccessfully. This consideration is not necessarily decisive, however, for the references need to be seen in the

---

[24] So Schanz 1904: 567. It may be significant that Victor styles Geiseric at the time of the invasion of Africa *dux* rather than *rex*, despite Geiseric having become king in 428 (*PLRE* 2: 497).

[25] Courtois 1954: 17-22; so too Constanza 1980: 246-49 and 1981: 16. Contra, Romano 1962: 21, 34.

context of a peroration which requests the presence of Catholics from across the whole world (3.64), not just the East, seeks the sympathy of brothers, and invokes the presence of the angels and the intercession of the patriarchs, prophets and apostles, especially Peter and Paul; indeed, the conclusion of the text could be held to have been addressed to the Roman church as plausibly as to anyone in Constantinople. Nor need we accept that Victor's failure to mention the disastrous expedition launched against the Vandals in 468 tells in favour of the thesis that he was writing a plea seeking Byzantine intervention:[26] rather, this matter was irrelevant to Victor's narration of a persecution. On the other hand, it is possible to read Victor's suggestion that anyone who found it hard to accept that people whose tongues had been cut out could still speak 'should go to Constantinople now'(3.30) as telling against this thesis, for this would have been a pointless recommendation to readers already in the city, and the implied criticism of Zeno's legate Uranius at 3.32 would hardly have been welcome in Constantinople (see too 2.5 for a further instance of implied criticism, and perhaps 2.38).

Such arguments, however, are not necessarily decisive, for it would be possible to construe criticism of Byzantine policy as an attempt to show that a firmer line was needed against the Vandals, and one consideration may be of weight. A brief passage in the *Codex Justinianus* published in 534, shortly after the triumphant conclusion of the war against the Vandals, describes the hardships which this people had caused the people of Africa in terms which could almost be read as a summary of Victor's narrative.[27] It is certainly possible that Victor's text circulated in Constantinople, but it is not necessary to credit Victor with having written with this in mind.

For the purpose of this translation I have not considered it necessary to evaluate variant manuscript readings in any systematic way, although the number of new readings proposed by Pitkäranta (1978) indicates that such a task could repay the attention of a

---

[26] So Courtois 1954: 51.

[27] *Codex justinianus* 1.27.2-4, where only the detail of churches having been turned into stables is foreign to Victor. Precise textual parallels are difficult to establish; the closest seems to be 'abscissis radicitus linguis' (*cod just* 1.27.4) and 'linguas...radicitusabscidisset' (Victor 3.30).

competent scholar. Of the two critical editions, those of Halm (*MGH AA* 3) and Petschenig (*CSEL* 7), I have generally found the former more satisfactory, although Petschenig's printing of a greater number of variant readings, his use of a larger number of manuscripts, and fuller indices, fruits of the enquiries which produced his massive study of 1880, are still of value. The reader can therefore assume that the translation which follows is, in all substantial respects, of the text printed by Halm, with the following major variants (the sign * indicates a reading printed in neither critical edition; I have not listed passages which I have silently repunctuated):

*	1.3	(Halm p. 2.18) impendebant, *not* impetebant
	1.8	(p. 3.24) valuerit, *not* valuerat
*	1.9	(p. 3.29) maiorum, *not* maiorem (cf. Courtois 1954: 42n.146)
	1.11	(p. 4.9) meatu, *not* metu (cf. Pitkäranta 1978: 23)
	1.21	(p. 6.15) alio, *not* alius
	2.29	(p. 19.23) moriendos, *not* moliendo
	2.31	(p. 20.9f) ponuntur et custodes postibus, *not* puniuntur et custodes fustibus
	2.98	(p. 38.24) prophetant, *not* prophetat
	3.4	(p. 40.26) *delete* novae
	3.19	(p. 44.24) quia, *not* qui
	3.23	(p. 45.26) materna, *not* aeterna
	3.25	(p. 46.11) totam per orbem, *not* tota die per orbem
	3.39	(p. 50.21) veredi, *not* viro
*	3.43	(p. 51.16) *omit* sacci sui
	3.45	(p. 51.30) sum, *not* sit
*	3.51	(p. 53.15) fecerant, *not* finxerant (cf. Pitkäranta 1978: 138)
	3.54	(p. 54.10) impio, *not* imperioso
	3.60	(p. 55.29) primam secunda, *not* prima secundam

To avoid a multiplication of footnotes I have supplied references to biblical quotations and allusions in parentheses, without troubling to register minor ways, whether due to the text which Victor or the authors of the *Book of the catholic faith* were familiar with, faulty memory, or some other cause, in which they differ from modern printed versions of the Bible. The chapter and verse numbers of the psalms are those of the Vulgate, but the names of books of the Bible are those by which they are generally known in English. Where 'Vulg' is added, the text Victor cites is similar to the Vulgate and differs significantly from the modern translations readers may have at their disposal; where 'cf' is added, Victor's text is significantly different from both the Vulgate and modern versions.[28] Similarly, I have sometimes supplied in parentheses the modern names of towns mentioned by Victor, using for this purpose the data gathered by Mandouze 1983 in the first place, and by Courtois 1954, to which I must record my indebtedness. I have at all times tried to keep in mind the obligation of a translator to render 'non verbum e verbo, sed sensum...de sensu,' and hope that this version will succeed in making a fascinating text better known.

---

[28] It must be said that some of the variants which occur in the *Book of the catholic faith* constitute amendments in a Trinitarian direction.

A HISTORY OF THE PERSECUTION OF THE AFRICAN PROVINCE IN THE TIMES OF GEISERIC AND HUNIRIC THE KINGS OF THE VANDALS, WRITTEN BY THE HOLY VICTOR THE BISHOP, WHOSE NATIVE PLACE WAS VITA[1]

PROLOGUE

1 In times past the ancients, led on by their desire for wisdom, kept on examining and enquiring carefully into the things which might have happened, for good or otherwise, in provinces, places or regions.[2] When they dealt with these matters they sharpened the pen of their intellect and offered to those ignorant of the floral gatherings of history the perfumed flowers of their teaching freely, as a gift. They saw to it that nothing which had been done in any area remained hidden.

2 But those people, puffed up with the arrogance of worldly love, longed for the glory of their haughtiness to be proclaimed and praised far and wide. You, on the other hand, being moved by the wish, so worthy of respect, to compose a history, conduct your affairs with a similar ardour indeed, but with a different love. They acted so as to be praised in this world, but you so that you might be seen as radiant in the world to come, and say: 'My soul shall rejoice in the Lord; let the gentle hear and be glad.' (Ps 33:3) You will be able to do as you have wished because you have received from heaven 'every good endowment and every perfect gift' (Jas 1:17), having been taught by a great pontiff who is worthy of being extolled with praise of every kind, the blessed Diadochus, whose numerous sayings concerning catholic dogma, shining like stars, are well known. And for you 'it is sufficient to attain to the

---

[1] The title given here represents a reconstruction made on the basis of incipits and explicits, although Costanza (1980: 230f, 1981:8) suggests *regis* for *regum*, hence 'of Geiseric and Huniric the king'.

[2] I accept the authenticity of this prologue, with Courtois 1954: 19 and Pitkäranta 1978: 14-16, against Petschenig 1880: 727-732.

learning of your teacher' (cf Matt 10:25), because it suffices for the disciple to be like his master.[3]

3 I see another Timothy, instructed from his earliest childhood in the sacred writings (cf. II Tim 3:15), as well as Luke, sublime and alert among men, a disciple of the apostle Paul and a doctor by profession.

4 So I, bending my neck in obedience to the person giving the order, shall attempt to reveal, in summary and brief fashion, the things which occurred in the regions of Africa as the Vandals raged. Like a rural labourer, with weary arms I shall collect gold from hidden caves, but I shall not hesitate to hand over something which still looks unrefined and disordered for it to be tested in the fire by the judgment of a craftsman who may be able to mint solidi from it.[4]

---

[3] This passage is addressed to bishop Eugenius of Carthage. Diadochus is the bishop of Photike whose one hundred chapters on spiritual perfection survive (ed. des Places, *SC* 5 bis; *PG* 65: 1167-1212). Marrou (1943) suggests that Diadochus met the clergy of Carthage, including Eugenius, the presumed addressee of the prologue, when he was taken there by the Vandals after a pirate raid; more plausibly, Courtois (1954: 21f) sees Eugenius as an easterner who came to Carthage with Zeno's legate Alexander (below 2.3)

[4] On the topoi here, Pitkäranta 1978: 18.

BOOK 1

1 It is evident that this is now the sixtieth year since the cruel and savage people of the Vandal race set foot on the territory of wretched Africa. They made an easy passage across the straits, because the vast and broad sea becomes narrow between Spain and Africa, which are separated by only twelve miles.[1]

2 A large number made the crossing, and in his cunning duke Geiseric, intending to make the reputation of his people a source of dread, ordered then and there that the entire crowd was to be counted, even those who had come from the womb into the light that very day. Including old men, young men and children, slaves and masters, there was found to be a total of 80,000. News of this has spread widely, until today those ignorant of the matter think that this is the number of their armed men, although now their number is small and feeble.[2]

3 Finding a province which was at peace and enjoying quiet, the whole land beautiful and flowering on all sides, they set to work on it with their wicked forces, laying it waste by devastation and bringing everything to ruin with fire and murders. They did not even spare the fruit-bearing orchards, in case people who had hidden in the caves of mountains or steep places or any remote areas would be able to eat the foods produced by them after they had passed. So it was that no place remained safe from being contaminated by them, as they raged with great cruelty, unchanging and relentless.[3]

---

[1] The Vandals seem to have crossed into Africa in May 429 (Courtois 1955: 155 n.2). Jordanes reports that seven miles separate Spain and Africa (*get* 167), but both he and Victor are probably wrong (Courtois 1955: 159 n.2).

[2] On the figure of 80,000, Goffart 1980: 231-34 is convincingly sceptical, against e.g. Courtois 1955: 215-17 and Orlandis 1987:32. Salvian felt that there were not many Vandals (*gub dei* 7.27f), and Zacharias considered that, at the end of their kingdom in Africa, they were few in number compared to the Romans (*hist eccl* 9.17). If Victor is indeed describing the crossing of the Vandals in 429 it is odd that he styles Geiseric *dux*, as he had become king in the preceding year (above p. xiv n.24).

[3] For the early ravages of the Vandals, see too Possidius *V Aug* 28 (parallels, which do not seem to me to be particularly strong, between this author and Victor are discussed by Capello 1937: 106f) and the sermon *de tempore barbarico ii* (*PLS* 3: 287-98). Note too a letter of bishop

4 In particular, they gave vent to their wicked ferocity with great strength against the churches and basilicas of the saints, cemeteries and monasteries, so that they burned houses of prayer with fires greater than those they used against the cities and all the towns.[4] When they happened to find the doors of a sacred building closed they were keen to open up a way with the blows of their hatchets, so that of them it could then rightly be said: 'They broke its doors in pieces with their axes as if they were in a forest of trees; they cast it down with axe and hatchet: they set your sanctuary on fire: they cast the tabernacle of your name to the ground and defiled it.' (Ps 73:5-7 Vulg)

5 How many were the distinguished bishops and noble priests put to death by them at that time with different kinds of torments, as they tried to make them give up any gold or silver belonging to themselves or the churches! And so that the things which were in their keeping would be brought forth more easily under the pressure of pain, they inflicted cruel torments a second time on those who produced things, asserting that they had produced a part but not the whole, and the more a person gave, the more they believed he had still more.[5]

6 Some had their mouths forced open with poles and stakes, and disgusting filth was put in their jaws so that they would tell the truth about their money. They tortured others by twisting cords around their foreheads and shins until they snapped. Devoid of mercy they offered many people sea water, others vinegar, the lees of olive oil, fish sauce and many other cruel things, while full wineskins were placed near their mouths. Neither the weaker sex, nor regard for nobility, nor reverence for the priesthood softened those cruel hearts; on the contrary, when

---

Capreolus of Carthage explaining his inability to attend the council of Ephesus, held in 431 (*PLS* 3: 295f).

[4] According to Possidius (*V Aug* 30), only three churches survived, those of Carthage, Hippo and Cirta.

[5] Augustine's correspondent bishop Honoratus of Thiaua raised the question of clergy being tortured for wealth they did not possess (Augustine *ep* 228.5, quoted in Possidius *V Aug* 30), and Procopius reports that the worst charge which could be made against Africans was that of having money and hiding it (*BV* 1.5.16f; note that clergy are not specifically mentioned here.) Persecution of bishops is reported by Prosper Tiro *chron s.a.* 437.

they caught sight of some officeholder worthy of honour, the wrath of their fury was thereupon increased.

7 I am unable to recount the number of the priests and men holding the rank of *inlustris* on whom they placed enormous burdens, as if they were camels or other kinds of baggage animals, and forced to walk using iron goads. Some of them breathed their last in wretched fashion under their burdens. Mature age and that greyness, worthy of veneration, which whitens the hair of the head so that it looks like shining wool, obtained no mercy from the enemy.[6] Indeed, in their barbaric frenzy they even snatched children from their mothers' breasts and dashed the guiltless infants to the ground.[7] They held others by the feet, upside down, and cut them in two from their bottoms to the tops of their heads; then it was, perchance, that captive Zion sang: 'My enemy said that he would burn my lands, kill my little children and dash my infants to the ground.' (cf II Kings 8:12)

8 In some buildings, namely great houses and homes where fire had been of less service to them, they smashed the roofs in pieces and levelled the beautiful walls to the ground, so that the former beauty of the towns cannot be deduced from what they look like now. And there are very many cities with few or no inhabitants, for after these events the ones which survive lie desolate; for example, here at Carthage they utterly destroyed the odeon, the theatre, the temple of Memoria and what people used to call the Via Caelestis.[8]

---

[6] On 'hospes' as 'enemy', Pitkäranta 1978:124.

[7] Verbal similarities between this passage and a portion of Rufinus of Aquileia describing the siege of Jerusalem in A.D. 70 are pointed out by Wynn 1990:189, an important study where other borrowings by Victor from this author are noted. 'Barbaric frenzy' is discussed at some length by Costanza 1984.

[8] It is difficult to assess the reliability of this passage. That there were many cities with few or no inhabitants is taken literally by Frend 1971: 62, although Victor hardly supports his thesis of a decline already in the Roman period. Within Carthage, archaeological work is not yet helpful (Clover 1982a: 19; Hurst and Roskams 1984: 44f). The temple of Memoria is recently discussed by Senay and Beauregard 1986; I cannot see that the data of Victor 3.17 tell against the destruction of the temple (with Belyaev 1972, against Courtois 1954: 41). It may be worth noting that the temple of Caelestis had been overthrown by Catholics before the arrival of the Vandals: Quodvultdeus *lib prom* 3.44.

9 To speak only of the most noteworthy things, in their tyrannical presumption they delivered over to their religion the basilica of the Ancestors where the bodies of SS Perpetua and Felicitas are buried, the basilica of Celerina and the Scillitani, and others which they had not destroyed.[9] But where there were some defensive works against which the hostility of their barbaric frenzy was unable to prevail, countless throngs were brought together at the walls of the towns. These they put to death with their savage swords, so that when the corpses had rotted away they were able, by means of the stench of the decaying bodies, to bring about the death of those whom they had not been able to approach because of the sheltering walls which protected them.

10 Who will be able to declare how many and how numerous were the bishops who were then tortured by them? For it was then as well that Pampinianus, the venerable bishop of our town,[10] was burnt all over his body by plates of glowing iron; in the same way Mansuetus of Urusi (Henchir Sougga) was burnt in the Porta Fornitana. At this time the city of Hippo Regius (Annaba), which the blessed Augustine, worthy of all praise, governed as its pontiff, was besieged.

11 Then that river of eloquence,[11] which flowed richly over all the fields of the church, dried up in the midst of its course, and the pleasant sweetness, so sweetly provided, was turned to bitter absinth, in accordance with the cry of David: 'When the sinner stood against me I became dumb and was abased, and kept silent even from good.' (Ps 38:2f Vulg) Until that time he had written 232 books, not including his letters, which are beyond counting, his exposition of the entire psalter

---

[9] For these basilicas, Courtois 1954: 42f and Clover 1982a: 9f; the basilica of the Ancestors is discussed by Frend 1977: 25f. Churches were used as stables in Vandal Africa, according to *cod just* 1.27.1.3, although it need not refer to this period.

[10] In other words, Pampinianus was bishop of Vita.

[11] The expression used here, 'flumen eloquentiae,' is employed by Quintillian *(inst orat* 10.1.61) as well as Augustine himself *(civ dei* 19.4). Victor subsequently applies the term 'eloquentiae fluvius' to Cicero (3.61).

and the gospels, and his sermons to the people which the Greeks call 'homilies', the number of which it is quite impossible to establish.[12]

12 Why say many things? After these wild and frenzied acts of wickedness Geiseric gained and entered Carthage, that great city, and reduced to slavery its old class of free men, freeborn and noble; for his captives included not a few of the senators of the city.[13] He thereupon published a decree that each person was to bring forward whatever gold, silver, gems and items of costly clothing he had, and so in a short time the greedy man was able, by means of this device, to carry away property which had been handed down from fathers and grandfathers.

13 He also made an arrangement concerning the individual provinces: Byzacena, Abaritana and Gaetulia, and part of Numidia he kept for himself; Zeugitana and the proconsular province he divided up as 'an allotted portion for his people' (I Chron 16:18); and he allowed Valentinian, who was still emperor, to take for himself the remaining, and now devastated, provinces.[14] After Valentinian died[15] he gained control of the coastline of all Africa, and with his customary arrogance he also took the large islands of Sardinia, Sicily, Corsica, Ibiza, Mallorca and Menorca, as well as many others.

---

[12] Augustine died on 28 August 430, during the Vandal siege of Hippo (Brown 1967: 432), although there is no need to connect his passing with the Vandals. The estimate of his output follows his own reckoning (*retract* 2.93, with *ep* 224.3, where there is the same gloss on 'sermons to the people').

[13] Carthage fell on 19 October 439; for Geiseric's activities there, Prosper Tiro *chron s.a.* 439.

[14] Victor's description of the division of Africa is confirmed by other classes of evidence: Courtois 1955: 218-20. Abaritana seems to have been to the south of Gaetulia, itself to the south of Numidia (Desanges 1963: 49-56). Zeugitana was another term for the proconsular province (*cod just* 1.27.1.12); Victor's use of 'et' immediately after 'Zeugitana' is therefore awkward, but cf below 1.29, 1.39. For the *sortes Vandalorum*, the establishment of which obviously involved the dispossession of the landowning class, see Procopius *BV* 1.5.12-15; Vandal settlement is discussed by Koenig 1981:340f. Valentinian III had become emperor in 425.

[15] Valentinian III was killed in Rome on 16 March 455.

14 One of these, namely Sicily, he later conceded to Odovacer, the king of Italy, by tributary right.[16] At fixed times Odovacer paid tribute to the Vandals, as to his lords; nevertheless, they kept back some part of the island for themselves. Moreover, Geiseric was by no means slow to enjoin the Vandals to put bishops and noble laity to flight from their churches and residences, completely naked. And if they were slow to leave when given the choice, they were to stay behind as perpetual slaves. This is something which happened to many people, for we know of many bishops and laity, *clari* and *honorati*, who are slaves of the Vandals.

15 But then he ordered that the bishop of the aforementioned city, that is, Carthage, a person well known to God and man, whose name was Quodvultdeus, and a great throng of the clergy, were to be placed naked on dangerous ships. Having been despoiled, they were to be driven away. In his merciful goodness the Lord graciously brought them to Naples, a town in Campania, after a safe passage. Geiseric badly treated a great number of senators and *honorati*, cruelly exiling them in the first place and subsequently driving them to lands beyond the sea.[17] When the bishop had been driven out, together with the venerable clergy, as we said above, he immediately delivered the church called Restituta, in which the bishops had always had their throne, over to his own religion, and he carried away all the churches which were inside the walls of the town, together with their wealth.[18]

16 But he also seized whatever churches he wanted to outside the walls, in particular two unusual and spacious ones dedicated to the holy martyr Cyprian, one where he shed his blood and the other where his

---

[16] Odovacer, spelt by Victor 'Odvacer', came to power in Italy in 476, and was murdered by Theoderic the Ostrogoth in 493.

[17] Exiles are discussed by Courtois 1955: 281f. Note the case of Gordianus, the grandfather of the theologian Fulgentius, one of the senators Geiseric forced to sail to Italy after they had lost all their wealth (*PG* 65: 119A). For Quodvultdeus, see Mandouze 1982: 949; his *lib prom* is extant (*SC* 101f).

[18] The carrying away of all the churches is hard to accept in the light of Victor 1.25. On the basilica Restituta, apparently the cathedral church, Courtois 1954: 43n.152. Koenig suggests, on the basis of Vandal names on epitaphs, that Augustine's cathedral at Hippo Regius was taken over by the Vandals (1981:341).

body is buried, at a place called Mappalia.[19] But who could put up with this, and be able to recall it without tears: he ordered that the bodies of our dead were to be taken for burial in silence, without solemn hymns.[20] More was to follow: the part of the clergy which still remained was also driven into penal exile.

17   While these things were going on, the remaining bishops and distinguished men of the provinces we have mentioned as having been divided up among the Vandals decided they would approach the king to implore his favour. When, in accordance with his custom, he had gone away to the shore of Maxula (Radès), which is commonly called Ligula, these people were seen coming to beseech him that, the churches and goods having been already lost, he give the people of God some comfort by allowing them at any rate the right to reside where the Vandals now held power.

18   It is established that that man replied to them through a messenger[21] with insane words: "I decreed that no-one of your reputation and birth was to be allowed to remain here, and you dare to ask for such things?" He even wanted to have them plunged into the nearby sea then and there, but his followers kept on asking him for quite some time not to do this. They went away consumed with sorrow and grief, and began to celebrate the divine mysteries in ways open to them and places where it was possible, their churches having been taken away. Thereafter, as the kingdom grew in wealth, the king's pride began to grow as well and to increase.

19 I shall mention something which happened at this time. There was a count Sebastian, subtle in counsel and valiant in war, son-in-law of

---

[19] See on these mysterious churches Ennabli 1975: 12-16; Duval 1982: 675-77.

[20] Pastorino suggests that Geiseric issued this order in the interests of public order (1980: 73f).

[21] I see no reason to translate 'internuntius' as 'interpreter', unlike e.g. Stein 1959: 320.

the well-known count Boniface.[22] Geiseric, just as he deemed his counsels necessary, dreaded being in his presence. He longed to put an end to him, and found a pretext for killing him in religion. The king decided to address Sebastian while his bishops and household officers were present. "Sebastian," he said, "I know that you have sworn to support us faithfully, and your toils and diligence show that your oath was true. But so that your friendship may always remain linked with us and constant, I have resolved, in the presence of our bishops, that you are to become a follower of the religion which we and our people venerate."

20 Sebastian devised something wonderful which would be useful for many people. He gave a wise reply in accordance with the circumstances: "Lord king, I beg that a loaf of the finest white bread be brought now." Geiseric, unaware of the victory Sebastian was to win, straightaway ordered that it be brought. Sebastian took the fine white bread and said: "To become so splendid and something considered suitable for the king's table, this bread, after the worthless bran was shaken from the heap of fine wheat flour, was sprinkled and passed through water and fire. For this reason it is considered fair to look at and pleasant to eat.

21 "In the same way I, ground in the mill of the Catholic mother[23] and cleansed like pure flour through the sieve of examination, was moistened by the water of baptism and cooked by the fire of the Holy Spirit. And through the agency of the divine sacraments God brought it about that I rose from the font pure, just like this bread from the oven. But, if it please you, let what I suggest be done. Let this bread be broken in pieces, moistened with water and made wet a second time, let it be put in the oven: if it comes out better, I shall do as you

---

[22] Sebastian's odd career is summarized in *PLRE* 2: 984. In 437 Geiseric put to death four of his advisers from Spain who refused to become Arians: Prosper Tiro *chron s.a.* 437; a letter from bishop Antoninus of Constantine to one of them is preserved: *PL* 50: 567-70. But in this case and that of Sebastian religion seems to have been a pretext rather than the point at issue.

[23] As do other authors, Victor sometimes omits the expected 'church' (cf e.g. Optatus 1.11, 7.6, *CSEL* 26: 14.3,178.7; Augustine *conf* 9.37; Victor 3.23.) Sebastian's speech makes no mention of the Trinity but turns on rebaptism, and thus anticipates a major theme of Victor's work. With this, compare the conclusion of *de tempore barbarico ii PLS* 3: 298.

suggest." Geiseric, when he and all those present had heard this proposal, was so entangled that it would have been impossible for him to have freed himself. Afterwards, on some other grounds, he had the warlike man put to death.[24]

22   But let us return to the point from which we digressed. By his deadly commands he caused terror, so that in the midst of the Vandals our people were quite unable to breathe. No place for praying or offering the sacrifice was conceded to these people in their grief, so that there was openly fulfilled the prediction of the prophet: 'In this time there is no prince or prophet or leader, nor a place to sacrifice to your name.' (Dan 3:38 Vulg) For every day saw fresh pieces of trickery which also affected those bishops who dwelt in regions which paid tribute to the palace. If perchance someone, as is the custom in sermons to the people of God, had named Pharaoh, Nabuchodonosor, Holofernis or someone similar, they accused him of having said such things against the person of the king, and immediately drove him into exile.[25] For this was the nature of the persecution being waged, here openly and there covertly. Their aim in using such pieces of trickery was to cause the name of the pious to perish utterly.

23   I knew many of the bishops who were banished for this reason, such as Urbanus of Girba, Crescens the metropolitan of the town of Aquitana, who presided over 120 bishops, Habetdeum of Teudalis, Eustratius of Sufes (Sbiba), and two bishops from Tripolitania, Vicis of Sabrata (Sabratah) and Cresconius of Oea (Tripoli), and also Felix the bishop of the town of Hadrumentum (Sousse), who had received a certain John, a monk, from overseas;[26] but there were also many others, of whom it would take long to tell. Nevertheless, when those who had been placed in exile died, others were not permitted to be

---

[24] Hydatius dates the death of Sebastian to 450 (*chron s.a.*).

[25] On sermons, see *PL* 42: 1122f (Herod), *PL* 51: 796, 810C, *PLS* 1: 288-94 (the Holy Innocents); see further Courcelle 1964: 137n.1; Courtois 1955: 286. It may not be accidental that the *lib prom* of the exiled Quodvultdeus discusses both Pharaoh and Nabuchodonosor, nor that Victor concludes the following chapter with a reference to the people of Israel under Pharaoh.

[26] Schmidt suggests that the monk was probably an agent of the Byzantine court (1942: 93).

ordained for their towns. Despite this, in the midst of these things the people of God remained steadfast in the faith, and, like a swarm of bees building dwellings of wax, it was strengthened as it grew with the honeyed pebbles of faith, so that there might be fulfilled that text: 'The more they afflicted them, the more they multiplied and grew in strength.' (Ex 1:12)

24 After these things had taken place, the supplication of the emperor Valentinian brought it about that, after the long silence of desolation, a bishop named Deogratias was ordained for the church at Carthage.[27] If anyone tried to itemize what the Lord did through him, he would run out of words before he could explain anything. But, after he had been made bishop, because of our sins it came to pass that Geiseric, in the fifteenth year of his reign, seized Rome, the city until then most noble and renowned. At that time he took into captivity the wealth of many kings, as well as people.[28]

25 When the throng of captives reached the shore of Africa, the Vandals and Moors divided the huge mass of people into groups.[29] Husbands were separated from wives and children from their parents, in accordance with the custom of barbarians. That beloved man who was filled with God busied himself immediately. He sold all the gold and silver vessels used in worship and freed the freeborn people from being slaves of the barbarians, so that spouses would remain together and children be returned to their parents. And because there were no places large enough to hold such a throng, he set aside the two sizeable

---

[27] Deogratias became bishop of Carthage on 24 October 454 (Mandouze 1982: 271).

[28] Geiseric's possible motives for the expedition against Rome in 455 are discussed by Courtois (1955: 19); the scale of the plunder is suggested by Procopius *BV* 1.5.3-5, 2.9.5 and Victor of Tunnunna *chron s.a.* 455. Almost a century later Jordanes described Geiseric as 'very well known' for his sack of Rome: *get* 168. See in general Béla (1979). It is a little odd to find the expedition to Rome dated to the fifteenth year of Geiseric's reign, for he had become king in 428. But the expedition occurred within the fifteenth year of the capture of Carthage, and Victor was probably using this mode of calculation, which accounts for his later attributing to Geiseric a reign of 37 years and three months (1.51). Procopius also used his entry into Carthage as a basis for reckoning (*BV* 1.7.30).

[29] On the Moorish tribespeople, see the contributions of M. Mahjoubi (pp. 491ff) and P. Salama (pp. 507ff) in Mokhtar 1981, and Whittaker 1978.

basilicas we have named, that of Faustus and that of the Novae, with beds and straw, deciding each day how much it was proper for each person to receive.[30]

26 Because most of them had been weakened by sailing, an experience with which they were unfamiliar, and by the harshness of their captivity, there was no small number of sick people among them. That blessed bishop acted like a good nurse. He continually went on rounds with the doctors, and food was brought behind him, so that when each person's pulse had been taken, that person might be given what was needed, in his presence. He did not even rest from this merciful work in the hours of night, but he went on, hurrying from bed to bed, enquiring as to how each was doing. So it was that he took on himself every burden, sparing neither his weary limbs nor his decayed old age.[31]

27 The Arians, inflamed by spite at this, used many tricks and frequently attempted to kill him. I believe that the Lord, in his foresight, wished to free his sparrow from the hands of those hawks quickly.[32] The captives brought from Rome bewailed his death, for this reason: when he went to heaven, they thought that they would be delivered into the hands of the barbarians. He had carried out the duties of bishop for three years. Moved by their love and desire for him, the people would have snatched the limbs of the worthy body had he not been buried when he died, and had not the multitude been kept in ignorance, in accordance with wise advice.

28 One should never remain silent concerning the wicked things done by the heretics, and there can be nothing shameful in something which contributes to the praise of one who suffers. So: one of those who had

---

[30] The basilica Fausti was the church in which Deogratias had been ordained bishop (Prosper Tiro, *chron cont cod reich* 25, *MGH AA* 11: 490.) Presumably it assumed the functions of a cathedral after the confiscation of the Restituta (above 1.15; Courtois 1954: 44; note that it is where Eugenius later performed the Epiphany baptisms (2.48-50) and that it is called 'ecclesia' below at 2.18 and 3.34, and the more general 'basilica' at 2.48.) Literary references to the basilica Novarum are provided by Courtois 1954: 43.

[31] For 'cariosa senectus', see Ovid *amor* 1.12.29.

[32] For the dating of the death of Deogratias to before the end of 457, Mandouze 1982: 271f.

ordained the abovementioned bishop, whose name was Thomas, was quite often harassed by their various plots. One day, in full view of everyone, they flogged the venerable old man. But he, considering that it was not a cause for shame but the price of his glory, rejoiced in the Lord.

29 So it came about that, after the death of the bishop of Carthage, they forbade the ordination of bishops for Zeugitana and the proconsular province. There used to be 164 of them, but little by little this number has diminished, and now they seem to number just three, if indeed these survive: Vincent of Zigga, Paul of Sinnari, truly a Paul in merit as well as name, and one other, Quintianus, who fled persecution and now lives as a foreigner at Edessa, a town in Macedonia.

30 But it is clear that there were also a great many martyrdoms and a huge and numerous throng of confessors; I shall try to tell a few things about them.[33] There were, at that time, some slaves who belonged to a certain Vandal, one of the Vandals called 'millenarii',[34] Martinianus, Saturianus and their two brothers, as well as a fellow slave, a noteworthy handmaid of Christ called Maxima, who was beautiful in both body and heart. And because Martinianus was the one who made his weapons[35] and always held in high regard by his lord, while Maxima was mistress over the entire household, the Vandal thought that he would unite Martianus and Maxima in marriage, in order to make these members of his household more faithful to himself.

---

[33] On the distinction between 'martyr' and 'confessor', Delehaye 1927: 74-121. At 3.21 Victor uses 'martyr' in the old sense of a witness to the faith in time of persecution, with a meaning similar to 'confessor', and note that Cyprian *epp*. 10 and 15 are addressed to 'martyrs and confessors.' Note in the following tale how Victor calls the chief catholic protagonists by their own names, whereas their antagonist is simply called 'Vandalus' or 'barbarus'.

[34] On the title 'millenarius', Claude 1971. Somewhat oddly, Diesner sees in the circumstances of this millenarius a transitional stage from a slave-owning to a feudal society (1966: 120).

[35] For the office of armourer, Cassiodorus *var*. 7.18f.

31 Martinianus, in the way of young men of this world, wanted to be married, but Maxima, who was already dedicated to God, had no desire for a human marriage. When they came to approach the quiet privacy of their bedroom and Martinianus, ignorant of what God had decreed for him, desired, with the boldness of a husband, to lie with her as with a wife, the abovementioned handmaid of Christ replied to him in a lively voice: "O brother Martinianus, I have dedicated the limbs of my body to Christ, and as there is a heavenly and true being to whom I am already betrothed, I cannot enter into a human marriage. But I shall give you some advice. If you want to, you as well will be able to gain him, while it is allowed, so that you too may have the delight of serving the one whom I have longed to marry."

32 So by the Lord's doing it came to pass that the young man was obedient to the virgin, and he too profited his soul.[36] While the Vandal remained ignorant of the spiritual secret they shared, Martinianus, feeling compunction and now a changed man, persuaded his brothers that, inasmuch as they were brothers, they should possess in common the treasure which he had found. And so, after his conversion,[37] he and his three brothers, accompanied by the maiden of God, secretly went forth by night to join the monastery of Tabraca (Tabarka), over which that noble shepherd Andreas then presided.[38] She went to live in a convent of maidens not far away.

33 The barbarian began to carry out an investigation. He made enquiries and distributed numerous gifts, and what had happened could not be hidden. So it was that, discovering them to be not his slaves but those of Christ, he threw the servants of God into chains and inflicted various torments on them, his purpose being not so much to make them have intercourse but, something worse, to make them defile the ornaments of their faith through the filth of rebaptism. This came to the notice of Geiseric. The king decreed that the implacable master

---

[36] The motif of an unconsummated marriage often occurs in early ascetic literature.

[37] 'Conversus' is used here in a sense approaching its medieval meaning of one who has become a monk in adult life.

[38] On monasticism in Vandal Africa, see Diesner 1964: 140-48.

was to keep afflicting his slaves for as long as it took for them to yield to his will. He ordered that strong cudgels were to be made which had jagged edges like palm branches, in the manner of saws: as these beat upon their backs they would not only break their bones but, as the spikes bored through them, would remain inside them.

34 As their flesh was torn in pieces the blood poured out and their inner parts were exposed to view, but on each occasion, as Christ healed them, they were restored unharmed on the next day. This happened quite often, over a long period, and no traces of their wounds were to be seen, the Holy Spirit curing them immediately. After this a harsh imprisonment was imposed on Maxima and she was cruelly stretched out on a 'spear'.[39] The throng of the servants of God who had been visiting her was still there and, as everyone looked on, the putrefaction caused by the enormous pieces of wood vanished. The voices of all made this miracle known, and the man responsible for her custody testified to me on oath that this is what happened.

35 But when the Vandal refused to recognize divine power, avenging grace began to operate in his house. He and his children died at the same time, and the best from among his household and his animals perished as well. The lady of the house was therefore left a widow, bereft of her husband, children and fortune, and she offered the servants of Christ as a gift to a relative of the king, Sersao. The latter received the people offered to him with joy, but a demon began to trouble his children and the members of his household severely with various disturbances on account of the holy ones. In turn, his relative reported to the king what had happened. Immediately the king decreed that they were to be sent to a king of the Moors, a pagan who bore the name Capsur; so it was that they were banished.[40] But he freed Maxima, the handmaid of Christ who had put him to shame and overcome him, to do as she wished. She lives on, a virgin and the mother of many virgins of God, and is by no means unknown to me.

---

[39] 'Cuspis', apparently the only use of this word by any Latin writer to designate an instrument of torture.

[40] See on the geography Courtois 1954: 37f, who suggests that Capsur's kingdom was in the region between Capsa (Gafsa) and Negrine.

The others arrived and were handed over to the king of the Moors we have mentioned, who was living in a part of the desert which is called Caprapicta.

36 The disciples of Christ, seeing the many forbidden and sacrilegious sacrifices carried out by the pagans, began by their preaching and way of life to invite them to the knowledge of the Lord our God, and by this means they gained an enormous multitude of pagan barbarians for the Lord Christ, in a place where the fame of the Christian name had hitherto been spread by no-one. Then they gave thought as to what should be done, so that the field which had now been cultivated and cleared of grass by the ploughshare of preaching might receive the seed of the gospel and be watered by the rain of holy baptism.[41]

37 They sent messengers across the long roads of the desert. At last they came to a Roman town[42] and the bishop was asked to send a priest and junior clergy to the believing people. The pontiff fulfilled their request with joy: a church of God was built, a great throng of barbarians was baptized all together, and from those who had been wolves an abundant flock of lambs was multiplied. Capsur sent a report of this to Geiseric. His ill will was aroused, and he ordered that the servants of God were to have their feet bound behind the backs of four running horses and perish together in the thorny places of the woods, the bodies of those innocent ones, as they were dragged to and fro, being cut to pieces by the spikes of the thorn bushes in the woods. He also ordered that they were to watch each others' deaths, one after the other.

38 When, in turn, they caught sight of each other, the unbroken horses running nearby as the Moors beat them, each one, in his difficult situation as the horses sped, said farewell in this fashion: "Brother, pray

---

[41] Verbal parallels between this section and a passage in Rufinus are pointed out by Wynn 1990:193.

[42] Augustine was aware of the failure of the Christian religion to penetrate the interior regions of Africa which were not under Roman power (*ep* 199.12.46; see too Optatus 3.3, *CSEL* 26:74). Leclercq (1904a: 179, 1904b: 358) is certainly wrong in taking the 'civitas Romana' to be Rome, and provides the sentence with papal connotations by so misunderstanding it.

for me; God has fulfilled our desire. This is the means by which the kingdom of heaven is reached." And so they sent forth their devout souls with prayer and psalms, as the angels rejoiced. Until this day our Lord Jesus Christ has not ceased to work mighty wonders there. For the blessed Faustus, a former bishop of Buruni (Henchir ed Dakhla), testified to me that a blind woman received her sight there in his presence.

39 After these happenings Geiseric was inflamed against the church of God. He sent one Proculus to the province of Zeugitana, to force the priests of the Lord to hand over the objects used in divine service and all the books. First the crafty foe took away their arms, so that when they were defenceless he would be able to capture them more easily. When they cried out that they would not hand these over, they took everything away with their greedy hands, and from the altar cloths, what wickedness! they made shirts and breeches for themselves. But Proculus, who carried this out, chewed up his tongue into little pieces and after a short time had passed suffered a most shameful death.

40 Then an order was given that the holy Valerian, bishop of the town of Abensa (Bordj-Hamdouna), who had struggled manfully so as not to hand over the things of God, was to be driven outside the town by himself, and it was decreed that no-one was to allow him to live in either a house or a field. For a long time he lay on a public road, in the open air. He was more than 80 years old, and despite my unworthiness I was privileged to be able to pay my respects to him while he was undergoing such an exile.

41 At one time when the solemnity of Easter was being celebrated, the Arians learned that our people had opened a church which had been shut at a certain place called Regia, so they could celebrate Easter Day. Straightaway one of their priests, whose name was Anduit, got together a band of armed men and incited them to attack the throng of the innocent. They went in with swords drawn, they snatched arms; others climbed onto roofs and fired arrows through the windows of the church. Just then, as the people of God were listening and singing, a

lector was standing on the platform chanting the Alleluia.[43] At that moment he was struck by an arrow in the throat. The book fell from his hand, and he himself fell backwards, dead.

42 It is known that many others were killed by arrows and javelins right in front of the altar, and those who were not slain by the sword received harsh treatment at the king's command and were nearly all put to death, especially those who were older. For elsewhere, as happened at Tunuzuda, Gales (Henchir el-Kharrouba), Vicus Ammoniae and some other places, at the time when the sacraments were offered to the people of God they went in wildly, scattered the Body and Blood of Christ on the floor and stamped on it with their filthy feet.

43 At that time Geiseric, urged on by his bishops, decreed that only Arians were to be placed in the various offices within his and his sons' court. This was the experience which then befell our Armogas, among others. Over a long period they frequently bound around his shins strings which made a jangling noise, and they ripped into his forehead, on which Christ had fixed the standard of his cross, so that it looked wrinkled, or rather ploughed, while they made noises as if they were animals. But as the holy man looked towards heaven the strings were broken as if they were the threads of spiders' webs. When the torturers saw that the strings which had bound him were broken, they kept on bringing stronger strings and pieces of hemp, but he simply invoked the name of Christ and they were all as nothing. Moreover, while he was made to hang with his head downwards, supported by one foot, everyone saw him sleeping as if he were on a feather bed.

44 The punishments had not been severe enough, and the king's son Theoderic, who was his lord, ordered that he be beheaded. But he was restrained by his priest Jucundus,[44] who said to him: "You have the power to kill him with torments of different kinds, but if you slay him with the sword, the Romans will begin to preach that he is a martyr."

---

[43] On the liturgical singing of the Alleluia in the season of Easter, Augustine *serm* 252.9.9.

[44] Jucundus' relationship with Theoderic was to bring him to a sad end; see below 2.13.

Then Theoderic condemned him to digging ditches for vines in the
province of Byzacena. Afterwards, as if to his greater shame, he
ordered that he was to be a cowherd not far from Carthage, where he
would be seen by everyone.

45 In the midst of these things Armogas perceived, by a revelation
from the Lord, that the day of his falling asleep was at hand. He
summoned Felix, a Christian worthy of reverence, the superintendent
of the household of the king's son and a man who venerated him as if
he were an apostle, and said to him: "'The time of my death is near.'
(II Tim 4:6) Of your kindness I entreat you, by the faith we both hold,
to bury me under this carob tree; if you do not do this, you will render
an account to our Lord." This was not because he cared where or how
his body was buried, but so that what God had revealed to his servant
might be made manifest.

46 Felix answered and said: "Far be this from us, venerable confessor!
I shall bury you in one of the basilicas in triumph and with the
thanksgiving which you deserve." The blessed Armogas replied: "No, do
as I have said." Fearing to make the man of God sad, he promised that
what he had ordered would, in truth, be done. Very shortly, within a
few days, he departed this life, accompanied by a good confession.[45]
Felix hastened to give him the burial he had commanded under the
tree. The intertwined roots and the hardness of the dry soil slowed him
down and he found the work painful, so that the burial of the limbs of
the holy body proceeded rather slowly. Finally, when the roots had
been cut back, they dug into the earth much more deeply and caught
sight of a sarcophagus, all ready and made of the most splendid
marble, such as, perhaps, none of the kings had had.

47 And I must not pass over a chief pantomime named Mascula. He
was harassed with many cunning traps to make him abandon the
catholic faith, and later the king himself invited him to do this, coaxing
him with worldly speech. He promised that great wealth would be

---

[45] Here, and later, 'confessio' means a confession, not of sin, nor of praise, but of faith.
For the use of this word in Augustine, see the note, by A. Solignac, to M. Skutella's edition of
the *Confessions*, Paris 1962 p. 11n.2.

heaped upon him, if he were to give a favourable hearing to what he wanted. But when he remained strong and unconquered in the faith, the king ordered that he was to undergo capital punishment. Nevertheless, in his cunning way he secretly enjoined that if, at that time, Mascula was frightened by the blow of the quivering sword, he was to be killed, so that he would not be turned into a glorious martyr; if, on the other hand, he remained strong in his confession, the sword was not to be used. But, with Christ giving him strength, he was made strong, like a column which could not be moved, and came back a glorious confessor. Even if the envious enemy refused to make him a martyr, nevertheless he was not able to inflict injury on our confessor.[46]

48 We know of another man of that time, whose name was Saturus. A shining member of the church of Christ, with catholic freedom he often reproved the Arians for their perversity; he was the superintendent of the household of Huniric. Saturus was cited on the complaint of one Marivadus, a deacon whom the wretched Huniric held in signal honour,[47] and it was decided that he was to become an Arian. Honours and wealth in abundance were promised if he did this; dire punishments were to be prepared if he refused. This was the choice placed before him: if he did not obey the king's commands, an examination was to be conducted. First of all he would lose his house and wealth, and all his slaves and children would be sold; then, while he was present, his wife would be given in marriage to a camel driver.

49 But he, filled with God, provoked those wicked people so that things would be set in train more quickly. For this reason his wife, without the knowledge of her husband, thought that she would seek some delay from those who were acting in the matter. Another Eve, directed by the counsel of the serpent, she came to her husband. But he was no Adam who would touch the alluring fruit of the forbidden

---

[46] A similar motif in Gregory of Tours *hist franc* 2.3, although here applied to bishop Eugenius. Gregory does not emerge well from a comparison of his data with those of Victor; see below at 2.47.

[47] Marivadus may plausibly be identified with a deacon against whom Vigilius of Thapsus wrote a book (*PL* 62: 226D, 351).

tree, because his name was not Needy[48] but Saturus, having been
saturated by the riches of the household of God and having drunk from
the torrent of his delights. (cf Ps 35:9) The wife came to a place
where her husband was praying by himself. She had rent her garments
and let down her hair; their children were with her and she carried in
her hands a little girl who was still at the breast. She placed her at the
feet of her unknowing husband, while she herself embraced his knees
with her arms and hissed with the voice of a snake:[49] "Take pity on
me, sweetest, and on yourself as well; take pity on the children we
share, whom you see here. Those whom descent from our stock has
made renowned should not be allowed to become slaves. And I should
not be subjected to an unworthy and shameful marriage while my
husband is alive, I who have always thought myself fortunate among
those of my age because of my Saturus. God knows that you will have
done against your will something which others may well have done
voluntarily".

50 That Job answered her with the voice of a saint: "'You are speaking
just as one of the foolish women.' (Job 2: 10)[50] I would be afraid,
woman, if the bitter sweetness of this life were the only thing. You are
the servant, wife, of the cunning of the Devil. If you loved your spouse,
you would never entice your own husband to a second death. Let them
sell the children, let them take my wife from me, let them carry away
all my wealth; trusting in his promises, I shall hold fast to the words of
my Lord: 'If anyone does not give up his wife, children, fields or house,
he cannot be my disciple.'" (cf. Luke 14:26) Why say more? His wife,
rebutted, went away with the children, and Saturus was strengthened
to receive his crown. He was examined, lost his property, was wearied
by punishments and sent away a beggar, forbidden to appear in public.

---

[48] Indigens.

[49] I have not sought to express in the translation the sibilant qualities of the speech of
Saturus' spouse.

[50] Rather than yielding to the tempting of his wife, as Adam did to that of Eve, Saturus
replies as Job did to his wife, who advised him to curse God and die (or, as translated in the
Vulgate, to bless God and die). On Job being a more appropriate role model than Adam,
compare a letter of bishop Antoninus (PL 50: 567).

They took everything from him, but they were not able to carry off the stole of baptism.

51 After these things Geiseric ordered that the church of Carthage was to be closed and its priests and junior clergy scattered and dispersed to different places of exile, because there was no bishop. Thanks to the supplication the ruler Zeno made through the patrician Severus, it was, with difficulty, opened again, and so they all returned from exile.[51] What he did in Spain, Italy, Dalmatia, Campania, Calabria, Apulia, Sicily, Sardinia, Bruttium, Lucania, Old Epirus and Greece, those who suffered there things which are to be lamented will better tell.[52] But let this now be the end of the persecution waged against us by Geiseric, with as much pride as cruelty. His reign lasted for 37 years and three months.

---

[51] The mission of Severus, which apparently occurred in 474 (Courtois 1954:54 n.231) and marked a more conciliatory phase in Byzantine policy towards the Vandals, is also known from Malchus *frag* 5, trans R. C. Blockley, *The fragmentary classicizing historians of the later Roman empire* Liverpool 1983 (= *frag* 3 according to the traditional enumeration), which provides fuller details. It is curious that in this passage Victor styles Zeno 'princeps' rather than 'augustus' or 'imperator'.

[52] Geiseric's ravages are known from Procopius *BV* 1.5.22f, 1.7.26. 1.22.16-18; Priscus *frag* 52 Blockley (= *frag* 40 according to the traditional enumeration); *V Dan styl* 56; Gregory of Rome *dial* 3.1; Nestorius *The bazaar of Heracleides* p. 379.

BOOK 2

1 Following the death of Geiseric, his eldest son, Huniric, succeeded his father.[1] In accordance with the subtlety of the barbarians, at the beginning of his reign he began to act in quite a mild and moderate fashion. This was particularly so with respect to our religion, so that meetings of the people were held even where it had previously been decided under king Geiseric that spiritual assemblies were not to take place. And, to show that he was a man of religion, he decreed that the Manichaean heretics were to be sought out with painstaking care.[2] He had many of these people burned, and he sold more of them for ships across the seas. He found that nearly all the Manichaeans were adherents of his religion, the Arian heresy, especially its priests and deacons; so it was that, the greater his shame, the more he was kindled against them.

2 One of them, a monk of theirs called Clementianus, was found to have a piece of writing on his thigh: 'Mani, the disciple of Jesus Christ.' The aforesaid tyrant seemed quite worthy of praise for this reason, but in one matter he gave cause for dissatisfaction: he gazed about eagerly and with a cupidity which could not be satisfied, and burdened the provinces of his kingdom with various pieces of trickery and taxes, so that of him in particular it was said: 'A king in need of revenues is a great trickster.' [3] At the request of the emperor Zeno and Placidia, the widow of Olybrius, he gave the church of Carthage freedom to

---

[1] Huneric succeeded Geiseric following the death of his father on 25 January 477. In the text I reproduce the spelling of his name given by Victor. Our author literally terms Huneric the elder (maior) son of Geiseric, but he knew of two other sons (below, 2.12). A similar usage occurs at 2.13 and 2.14.

[2] The Manichaeans were disciples of Mani, a dualist teacher of the third century.

[3] Luxorius, writing later under the Vandals, composed two epigrams on Eutychus, the extortionate servant of a Vandal king (55f, ed Rosenblum p. 144); note in particular the motto 'regis habenda.'

ordain for itself whomever it wished as bishop. At that time the church had been deprived of such an ornament for 24 years.[4]

3 So it was that he now sent to the church the *vir inlustris* Alexander, to discharge an embassy to this effect: in his presence, the catholic people was to seek for itself a worthy bishop. He also sent, through his notary named Vitarit, an edict to be read out in public. Its contents were as follows: "The Lord orders this to be said to you. Because the emperor Zeno and the most noble Placidia have written through the *vir inlustris* Alexander seeking that the church of Carthage may have a bishop proper to your religion, he orders that this is to be done.

4 "He has written back to them and ordered that the legates sent by them are to be told that you are to go ahead and ordain the man you want as your bishop, in accordance with what they have sought. There is one condition: the bishops of our religion who are at Constantinople and throughout the other provinces of the East are to have, at his command, the right to preach to the people in whatever languages they wish in their churches[5] and to practise the Christian religion, just as you will have this right, here and in the other churches which are in the provinces of Africa, to celebrate mass, preach and do the things which pertain to your religion, in whatever way you wish.[6] Now, if this is not observed concerning them, the order is given for both the bishop who will have been ordained and the clergy, together with the other bishops with their clergy who are in the African provinces, to be sent among the Moors."

---

[4] The mission of Zeno's legate Alexander is known from Malchus *frag* 17 (ed Blockley; *frag* 13 according to the traditional enumeration); on the date see below n.8 to 2.6. Zeno was emperor from 474 to 491; Placidia, a daughter of the emperor Valentinian III (above 1.13), had been among the captives Geiseric took from Rome in 455, and was sent from Africa to Constantinople in c.461 (references in *PLRE* 2: 887).

[5] On the use of the vernacular among barbarian peoples converted to Christianity, John Chrysostum in *PG* 85: 501. It is possible to see adherence to Arianism and to a non-classical language as statements of identity by culturally insecure barbarian peoples.

[6] The uncoordinated structure of this passage is typical of the style of Huneric's edicts reproduced by Victor. In the interests of lucid English I have broken one sentence of the Latin into two.

5 I was present on 18 June when the edict was read to the whole church, and we began to groan softly, because the cunning plots of evil men had laid the ground for persecution in the future. And it is well known that the legate was told: "If this is so, and these dangerous conditions are put forward, it does not please this church to have a bishop, for Christ, who has always been pleased to govern it, governs it still." The legate paid no attention to what we said. At this the people flared up like a fire for things to go ahead then and there; their cry was insufferable, and no arguments were able to quieten them down.

6 The ordination of Eugenius, a holy man pleasing to God, as bishop produced the greatest delight, and the joy of the church of God was complete.[7] The catholic multitude rejoiced that they had been given the right to ordain a bishop again while the barbarians held power. For a great number of youths and young girls, sharing the joy they had in common, affirmed that they had never seen a bishop presiding from his throne. Henceforth bishop Eugenius, that man of God, began, thanks to his practice of good works, to be considered worthy of veneration and reverence even by those who were outside his flock, and such was the favour he enjoyed with everyone that, if it had been right, each person would have delighted to lay down his life for him.

7 The Lord was also pleased to bring about through him the giving of alms on such a scale that his expenditure seemed unbelievable, considering that the resources of the church, at a time when the barbarians held everything, were down to the last sesterce. If anyone were to begin, he would be unable to give a full account of the humility that was his, of his charity, and of the goodness bestowed on him by divine providence. It is well known that money never stayed with him, unless it happened to have been offered at the time when the sun, at the completion of the course of the day, yields and gives place to the darkness of the night. He kept as much as would suffice for a day, not

---

[7] Eugenius became bishop in 480/81, the see having been vacant since the death of Deogratias in 456/57 (Mandouze 1982: 362). His name suggests a Greek origin, and Courtois suggests that he came to Carthage with Zeno's legate Alexander (1954: 21f), although this seems a little strained.

as much as greed would have desired, and daily our God gave him large, and still greater things.

8 But when his reputation had spread everywhere and was generally known, the bishops of the Arians, especially Cyrila, began in consequence to be afflicted with a great deal of jealousy. Each day they railed at him with false accusations. Why say more? They made a proposal to the king concerning him, that he should on no account preside from his throne and preach to the people of God as usual; and then, that he should forbid the entry of any men or women in barbarian clothes who were seen going into the church. That man replied, as was right, "The house of God is open to all, and no-one should turn away people going in." This was especially so because a huge number of our Catholics who served in the royal household used to go in dressed like Vandals.

9 When the king received this answer from the man of God, he ordered that torturers were to be stationed at the entrances to the church; when they saw a woman or man who looked like one of their race going there, they were straightaway to thrust tooth-edged stakes at that person's head and gather all the hair in them. Pulling tightly, they took off all the skin from a person's head, as well as the hair. Some people, when this happened, immediately lost their eyes, while others died just from the pain. After this punishment the women, their heads stripped of skin, were paraded through the streets, with heralds going before them, so that the whole town could see. But they preferred to count those things which they suffered as their great gain. I became acquainted with very many of them, and I do not know of one who abandoned the right path, even under the impact of these punishments.

10 Being unable to break down the wall of faith in this way, he decided that the people of our religion who held positions at his court were to receive neither their rations nor their usual pay. Then he proceeded to wear them down with work in the country, sending freeborn and quite delicate men to the fields around Utica, to cut away the sods of the harvest under the fire of the burning sun. They all proceeded there with joy, rejoicing in the Lord.

11 In their company there was a man with a withered hand which had
been of no service to him for many years. When he, in all truth,
excused himself as being unable to work, he was the more violently
ordered to proceed. But when they reached the place and all groaned
in prayer, especially for him, by divine goodness the confessor's hand
was restored, in good condition. From this point the persecution of
Huniric, which was to bring us sorrow and travail, took its beginning.

12 This man, who had until then shown himself mild to everyone,
wished to assign the kingdom to his sons after his death; as it happened
this did not come to pass. He began to persecute in a cruel fashion his
brother Theoderic and the children of this man, and equally the
children of his brother Genton.[8] Not one of these would he let go,
unless death carried out what he desired. First of all, the tyrant ordered
that, after a charge had been laid against her, the wife of his brother
Theoderic, a woman he knew to be cunning, was to be killed with the
sword; I believe that this was in case she should arm her husband and
their elder son, who seemed sensible and wise, with more pointed
counsels against the tyrant.

13 Afterwards that son, who had received a higher education,[9] was
killed as well; to him in particular, according to the enactment of
Geiseric, the chief rule was due among his nephews, because he was
the eldest of them all. He was then stirred up to do something still
more cruel. He ordered that a bishop of his religion named Jucundus,
whom they called the patriarch, was to be consumed by fire in the
middle of the town on the steps of the new square, as the people stood
by. This was because he had been a most welcome visitor in the house
of the king's brother Theoderic, and with his assistance the
aforementioned house would, perhaps, have been able to obtain the
office of king. In this wicked crime we perceived that the evil which
was going to befall us was close at hand, and we said to one another:

---

[8] On succession arrangements among the Vandals, Courtois 1955: 238ff. Details of the
constitutio of Geiseric, mentioned by Victor in the following paragraph, are provided by Jordanes
get 169 and Procopius *BV* 1.7.29.

[9] Riché 1976: 64 discusses the openness of Vandal aristocrats to classical culture.

"How is a man who has come to be so cruel towards his own bishop going to spare our religion and us?"

14 Then he sent into exile Godagis, the eldest son of Genton, together with his wife, without a slave or handmaid to help them. In the same way he exiled his brother Theoderic, naked and in want, after his wife and son had been murdered. After Theoderic died he drove far away in affliction his surviving little son and his two grown-up daughters, seated on asses. But he also harassed very many counts and nobles of his race with false charges, because they were supporters of his brother. He had some burned, and he cut the throat of others, showing himself an imitator of his father Geiseric, who drowned the wife of his brother by throwing her, tied to heavy stones, into the well-known Amsaga River at Cirta (Constantine), and went on to kill the children after the death of their mother.[10]

15 Now his father Geiseric, as he was dying, had commended many people to Huniric, making him swear an oath; but that man, unmindful of his good faith and in violation of the oath, slaughtered these people with tortures of different kinds and with fires. For he shamefully beheaded one Heldica, whom his father had made superintendent of his kingdom and who was now an old man of many years, and he had his wife burned, together with another woman called Teucharia, in the middle of the town. He ordered that their bodies were to be dragged through the lanes and streets; only in the evening, after they had been lying a whole day, did he reluctantly agree to the request of his bishops and allow them to be buried. He was not able to kill Gamuth, the brother of Heldica, because he had taken refuge in one of their churches; nevertheless he shut him up in the cesspits, and ordered that he remain in that dirty place for a long time.

16 Afterwards he condemned him to dig ditches to be used for the planting of vines, in the company of a certain goatherd and a country fellow. In addition, he had them set about with harsh whips twelve

---

[10] These would have been the wife and children of Gunderic, who died in 428 and was succeeded as king of the Vandals by his half-brother Geiseric. The new king's activities against his family are known from no other source.

times a year, that is, on a monthly basis, and they were scarcely allowed
a drink of water or bread to eat. For five years or more they endured
this, men for whom their sufferings would have sufficed to obtain an
eternal reward if they had been Catholics who endured these things
because of their faith. But this has not led us to keep quiet about it,
and pass over in silence the wickedness of the king towards his own
people as well. Not only did he commit his bishop Jucundus to the
flames, as we have shown above, but he also had very many priests and
deacons of his, that is, Arians, burned and delivered to the beasts.

17 Having therefore in a short time disposed of all those he feared
and made his reign secure, as he thought, although it was to be brief
and transitory, and being thoroughly at leisure and free of trouble,
'roaring like a lion' (cf Ps 21:14) he turned all the missiles of his rage
towards a persecution of the catholic church. Nevertheless, prior to the
time[11] of persecution, the evil which impended was revealed by the
many visions and signs which preceded it.

18 Some two years before it took place, someone saw the church of
Faustus shining with its usual adornments of shining candles, cloth
coverings and glowing lamps. And while he was taking delight in so
radiant a splendour, suddenly, he said, the light, so wonderfully bright,
was extinguished, and in the darkness which followed there arose a
stench terrible to smell; and all the throng of the blessed was driven
outside by threatening Ethiopians. That he would never see the church
restored again to its original brightness was something to be lamented
without ceasing. I was present when he related that vision to the holy
Eugenius. And a priest saw that same church of Faustus crammed with
throngs of people beyond counting; a little while later it was empty,
and then it was filled again with a multitude of pigs and nanny-goats.

19 Likewise, someone else saw a threshing floor of wheat ready for the
winnowing, the grains having not yet been separated from the chaff in
accordance with the judgment of the winnower. And while he was

---

[11] 'Tempestas', although the original meaning of 'storm' would also be appropriate here.
According to Victor of Tunnunna, Huneric's persecution, more savage than that of his father,
was excited two years after he became king (*chron s.a.* 466).

marvelling at the size of the huge mass still mixed together, suddenly, behold! a whirlwind approached with a stormy noise which could be heard far away, and the dust rose as it began to make its presence felt. Under its impact all that chaff flew about, but the grains remained. Afterwards there appeared an impressive figure, his face shining and his bright attire gleaming. He began to cast forth the grains which were empty, thin and no good for flour, clearing them away. He spent a long time carefully going through that enormous mass; when he had put it to the test it was reduced to a tiny pile.

20 Likewise, someone else said: "A certain person who towered above Mount Ziquense was crying out to right and left 'Go away, go away!'" Someone else caught sight of sulphurous clouds in a thundering, turbulent sky which began to throw down huge stones. When these stones had fallen onto the ground they were kindled the more and burned with greater flames; they went inside houses and set the people they encountered on fire. The person who saw this said that when he had hidden himself in a bedroom, by divine mercy the blaze was not able to reach him, and I think that this was so that this prophecy would be fulfilled: 'Shut your door and hide for a while, until the wrath of God passes.' (Is 26:20)

21 And the venerable bishop Paul saw a tree which reached to the heavens with its flowering branches, big enough to cover almost all Africa with its shade. And while everyone was rejoicing at its size and beauty, behold, suddenly, he said, there came a savage donkey which rubbed its neck over the bottom of the trunk, and as it shoved it knocked that wonderful tree to the ground with a mighty noise.

22 The honourable bishop Quintianus saw himself standing on a mountain from which he could see the flock of his innumerable sheep, and in the middle of the flock were two pots, boiling fiercely. But there drew near people who slew the sheep and plunged their flesh into the boiling pots. And in the course of this, all that enormous flock was destroyed. I think that those two pots are the two towns Sicca Veneria (Kef) and Lares (Henchir Lorbeus), in which the multitude was first brought together and from which the fire took its beginning, or else

king Huniric and his bishop Cyrila. But I must be brief, so may it be enough to have said this much concerning the many visions.

23   Why say more? First of all the tyrant decreed, in a dreadful command, that no-one could hold an office in his palace or carry out public duties without becoming an Arian. There was a great number of people in these positions who, unconquered in their strength, abandoned temporal office so that they would not lose their faith; afterwards they were cast out of their homes, despoiled of all their possessions, and banished to the islands of Sicily and Sardinia. On one occasion he hurriedly issued a decree throughout all Africa that the fisc was to claim as its own the possessions of our dead bishops, and that the successor of a dead bishop could not be ordained until he had paid 500 solidi to the royal fisc.

24   But where the Devil strove to erect this building, straightaway Christ saw fit to pull it down. His household officers pointed out to him: "If your precept gives sanction to this, our bishops who are in the territory of Thrace and other regions will begin to suffer worse things." Thereafter he ordered that the consecrated virgins were to be gathered together, and sent the Vandals, with the midwives of his race, to examine and feel their private parts, contrary to the laws of modesty, when neither their mothers nor any women at all were present.[12] They tortured them by hanging them in a cruel way and tying heavy weights to their feet; they applied glowing plates of iron to their backs, bellies, breasts and sides.

25   While they were enduring these sufferings they were told: "Say that the bishops and your clergy used to go to bed with you." We know that very many of them died then because of their harsh punishments; others, who survived, were bent over because their skins were dried out. For he strove to find a path which would give him an opening for launching a persecution, as he in fact did. But by doing this he was unable to find any way to dishonour the church of Christ.

---

[12]   Surely the Vandal midwives (obstetrices) were women?

26 But with what floods of tears shall I proceed? He sent bishops, priests, deacons and other members of the church, to the number of 4,966, to exile in the desert.[13] Among them were very many who had gout, and others who had lost their worldly sight through age. Among their number was the blessed Felix, bishop of Abbir (Henchir el-Khandaq), who had then been a bishop for 44 years; having been struck with the disease of paralysis he did not feel anything, nor was he capable of speech.

27 We gave deep thought to this person, because he could not be carried on a beast of burden, and we suggested that the king be asked by his people to order that this man, soon to die, remain at Carthage, because there was no way in which he could be taken into exile. The tyrant is said to have spoken in a rage: "If he cannot sit on an animal, let untamed bulls be yoked to take him where I have ordered by dragging him along, fastened with ropes." We bound him crossways on a mule like the trunk of a tree, and in this manner we carried him with us for the whole journey.

28 Everyone was brought together in the towns of Sicca and Lares so that the Moors, who came to meet them there, would lead them to the desert after they had been handed over.[14] Two counts came up, and with damnable cunning they began to talk with the confessors of God in smooth words. "Why does it seem good to you," they said, "to be so stubborn, and why are you disinclined to comply with the orders of our Lord? For you would be considered worthy of honour in the sight of the king if you were to hurry to act in accordance with his will." Immediately they cried out and said with loud voices: "We are Christians, we are Catholics, we confess the Trinity, one God inviolable." They were shut up in a place of custody which, while

---

[13] Victor of Tunnunna mentions that about 4,000 were banished, including monks and laity (chron s.a. 479). Geographical aspects are examined by Courtois 1954: 38f.

[14] It is interesting to observe that Justinian was to erect defensive buildings to deal with the Moors at Sicca: Procopius build 6.7.10.

unpleasant, was still fairly spacious, and we were able to go in and give the brothers words of advice and celebrate the divine mysteries.[15]

29 There were many little children in that place, and their mothers followed them with maternal affection, some rejoicing and others summoning their children back; for some rejoiced that they had given birth to martyrs, while others strove to call back from the confession of faith those who would die from the deluge of rebaptism. Nevertheless, their coaxing words defeated no-one, and ties of the flesh made no-one bend to the ground. And it is with pleasure that we give a brief account of what one old woman did then.

30 When we were making our way in the company of the army[16] of God and generally advancing by night because of the heat of the sun, we caught sight of a little woman carrying a little sack and other garments, holding by the hand a little child[17] whom she was encouraging with these words: "Run, my lord; you see how all the holy men are moving forward and hastening, full of gladness, towards their crowns." And when we rebuked her, because she did not seem fit on the grounds of her sex to be in the company of men or to be associated with the army of Christ, she replied: "Give your blessing, give your blessing, and pray for me and this little grandson of mine, because even though a sinner I am the daughter of a former bishop of the town of Zura." We said to her: "And why do you walk in such a mean fashion, and why, as it appears, have you come on such a long journey here?" And she replied: "I am going into exile with this little one, your servant, lest the enemy come upon him all alone and call him back from the way of truth to death." At these words we were filled with tears and could say nothing other than "May God's will be done."

31 The enemy was perhaps already saying 'I shall divide the spoils, I shall fill my soul, I shall kill with my sword, my hand shall have

---

[15] From this it appears that, while Victor accompanied the confessors, he was not of their number. Leclercq 1904b: 373 twists the Latin badly to make him a confessor.

[16] 'Exercitus' is used elsewhere by Victor in the sense of 'people' (1.13, 3.60), which is a possible translation here.

[17] Note the use of diminutives here.

dominion' (Ex 15:9), but when he found himself unable to catch a single one he sought out cramped and exceedingly loathsome places, so that he could narrowly confine the army of God in these enclosed areas. Then they were even denied the consolation of visitors, for guards with cudgels were placed at the doors and beat them harshly, and as there was so little space the confessors of Christ were thrown one on top of the other, like hordes of locusts and, to use an appropriate term, the most precious grains of some crop.

32 Crowded together in this way, there was no room for people to step aside to answer the call of nature, and so they excreted and urinated when they had to, just where they were, so that the filth and horror of it were worse than any kind of punishment. With some difficulty we were once allowed to go in secretly, after we had given enormous gifts to the Moors and while the Vandals were asleep. Entering something like the abyss of a mire, we began to be immersed up to our knees, and saw that the statement of the prophet Jeremiah had then been fulfilled in that place: 'Those who were raised on saffron have embraced their own excrement.' (Lam 4:5) Why say more? With the Moors making a loud noise on every side, the order was given to prepare them for the journey which had been settled on for them.

33 And so they went forth on a Sunday, their clothes, together with their faces and heads, smeared with excrement. Although they were cruelly treated by the Moors, they sang with joy a hymn to the Lord: 'This is glory for all his saints.' (Ps 149:9) It was then that the blessed pontiff Cyprian, the bishop of Unizibir, approached them. An excellent comforter, he encouraged them individually with an affectionate and fatherly kindness, not without rivers of flowing tears, prepared to 'lay down his life for the brothers' (I Joh 3:16) and of his own accord to deliver himself up to like sufferings, if he were allowed. He spent all that he had on his needy brothers in their present necessity, for he sought a way of being associated with the confessors, being a confessor himself in spirit and virtue. Subsequently, after many contests and squalid times in prison, he proceeded with joy to his longed for exile.

34 The roads and paths bear witness to the size of the throngs of people from various regions and towns who ran to meet the martyrs of

God; these were by no means large enough for the mass of people on the move, who ran together across the tops of the mountains and along the valleys. A throng of the faithful too large to count came down. Carrying candles in their hands and casting their little children at the feet of the martyrs they cried out, saying: "To whom are you leaving us, wretches that we are, while you go on your way to crowns? Who is going to baptize these little ones in the font of ever-running water? Who will bring us the gift of penance and loose those bound by the chains of sins with the absolution of reconciliation?[18] For to you it was said, 'Whatever you loose on earth will be loosed in heaven.' (Matt 18:18) Who will bury us with solemn prayers when we die? By whom will the usual rite of the divine sacrifice be offered? Were it permitted, we would like to go forth with you, so that there would be no need for the children to be separated from their fathers."

35 While they were saying these things and crying, no-one was allowed to go forward to console them, but the throng was forced to move quickly, so that they would be able, with difficulty, to take up a lowly lodging where some poor accommodation had already been prepared. When the elderly and others, such as delicate youths, happened to falter, they started to find themselves being struck with the points of spears and stones to make them run, and the weaker they were the more weary they became.

36 But later, the order was given to the Moors that they were to tie together the feet of those who could not walk and drag them, like the corpses of dead animals, through harsh and bitter stony places, where first their clothes and then their limbs were torn off one by one, because of the swordlike sharpness of the stones. In one place a head was smashed, while in another ribs were split, and so they breathed out their spirit amid the hands of those who were dragging them. We have been quite unable to establish how many of them there were, their very

---

[18] The usage of 'reconciliation' in this sense is common in the African councils; see *CCSL* 259: 419, *sub verbis* 'reconciliare' and 'reconciliatio'.

number preventing it; nevertheless, all along the public road mean graves were raised for the holy ones, as the burial mounds tell us.[19]

37   The remainder, who were more fit, arrived at the uninhabited places, and when they were there they received barley to eat, as if they were beasts of burden.[20] It is said that there was such a large number of poisonous animals and scorpions there that it would seem unbelievable to those who do not know about it; these are creatures which, by their breath alone, pour poisonous venom even on those far away. And they say that no-one has ever survived the attack of a scorpion. But we have learned that, up to the present time, the savageness of their poison has not harmed one of Christ's servants, thanks to his defence of them. And whereas at first they were fed with grains of barley, later even this was taken away - as if God, who caused manna to rain on the fathers, was not able as well to provide food for those now subjected to the same kind of exile![21]

38   The tyrant turned his mind to more violent actions against the church of God, so that having cut off some of the limbs he could destroy the whole body by tearing it in pieces. For on the day of the Ascension of the Lord,[22] in the presence of Reginus, the legate of the emperor Zeno, he sent to bishop Eugenius an edict which was to be read out in the middle of the church. Its contents were as follows; he also forwarded it, by speeding post horses, to the whole of Africa.[23]

39   "Hunirix, king of the Vandals and Alans, to all the homousian bishops.[24] It is well known that not once but quite often your priests

---

[19] The relevance to this of the Uppena mosaic (ed Fiebiger, *Inschriftensammlung* 1939 no. 15, = *CIL* 8: 23 041), accepted by Courcelle (1964: 191n.3, with plate 13), has been denied by Courtois 1955: 295n.17 and, by implication, Duval 1982: 59-67.

[20]   But cf Procopius *BV* 2.6.13 on the diet of the Moors.

[21]   The rain of manna on the Israelites is described in Ex 16 and Num 11.

[22]   20 May 483.

[23]   On the post horses, Diesner 1968.

[24]   Wolfram 1967: 78, in the context of a discussion of the significance of this form of words for intitulature, argues for the authenticity of this document and another reproduced below (Victor 3.3-14) because of the spelling 'Hunirix', contrary to Victor's customary

have been forbidden to celebrate any liturgies at all in the territory of
the Vandals, in case they seduce Christian souls and destroy them.
Many of them have despised this and, contrary to the prohibition, have
been discovered to have said mass in the territories of the Vandals,
claiming that they hold to the rule of the Christian faith in its fullness.
And because we do not wish for scandal in the provinces granted us by
God, therefore know that by the providence of God and with the
consent of our holy bishops we have decreed this: that on the first of
February next you are all to come to Carthage, making no excuse that
you are frightened, so that you will be able to debate concerning the
principles of faith with our venerable bishops and establish the
propriety of the faith of the Homousians, which you defend, from the
divine scriptures. From this it will be clear whether you hold the faith
in its fullness. We have sent a copy of this edict to all your fellow
bishops throughout Africa. Given on 20 May 483 in the seventh year
of Hunirix."

40 As soon as those of us who were present came to know this as it
was read out, 'our heart was forthwith broken and our eyes grew dim'
(Lam 5:17), and in truth, 'the days of our festival were turned to
sorrow and our songs to lamentation'(Amos 8:10), since the contents
of the edict revealed that a raging persecution was to come, especially
where it said 'we do not wish for scandal in the provinces granted us
by God,' as if it were saying 'we do not wish there to be Catholics in
our provinces.' We discussed what was to be done. No remedy for the
calamity which threatened was to be found, except for the proposal, a
reasonable one were it possible for a barbarian's heart to be softened,
made by the holy Eugenius. The text follows.

41 "Whenever a discussion is held concerning the soul, eternal life and
the Christian faith, it is necessary that the subject of the enquiry be
dealt with without fear, just as the royal providence has promised. The

---

'Huniricus' (but note that he uses 'Hunirix' at 3.17.) One cannot help noticing that the form
'Rex Hunirix' is scarcely euphonious. See further on the chancellery of the Vandal kings
Heuberger 1929. For the later king Gelimer as 'king of the Vandals and Alans', see an
inscription ed. Fiebiger/Schmidt (1919 no.51, = *CIL* 8: 17 412) and Procopius *BV* 1.24.3, and
note too the title of the *Laterculus regum Wandalorum et Alanorum*.

royal power has recently seen fit to admonish my humble self through the notary Vitarit, who recited his edict dealing with religion and faith in the church, in the presence of the clergy and people. We learned from its contents that the royal order has similarly been sent out to all my fellow bishops, so that they may come together to dispute concerning the faith on the given date. This, have we advised, is to be respectfully obeyed. My humble self proposed to the aforesaid notary that he should recognize my colleagues, including those of all the regions across the sea, who are united with us in one religion and communion, because all people everywhere comply with his authority, and in particular because this is an affair of the whole world, not merely of the African provinces alone.[25]

42 "And because I promised in a subsequent reply that I would offer a proposal, with proper humility I ask your magnificence that he see fit to convey my aforementioned proposal to the ears of the lord and most clement king. So it will be that his clemency may realize that we by no means decline to dispute concerning religion with the help of God, nor do we avoid this, but we should not undertake the task of defending our faith without the agreement of the whole body. We ask that he may see fit to approve this, with that liberality which renders him so great and the justice of his wisdom. Given by Eugenius, bishop of the catholic church at Carthage."

43 But when this proposal was put forward by the blessed Eugenius, he who had 'already conceived anger' was now the more seriously driven to 'give birth to iniquity.' (Ps 7:15) So it was that he commanded the holy man, bishop Eugenius, through Obadus, the superintendent of his kingdom: "Subdue unto me the whole world so that all the earth is brought under my power, Eugenius, and I shall do what you say." To this the blessed Eugenius replied as best he could. "Something which has no sense," he said, "should not have been uttered. This is like saying to a man that he should be carried through the air and fly, which is not in accordance with human nature. For I said that, if in his

---

[25] Diesner (1966: 79f) suggests that Eugenius sought to turn the meeting into an ecumenical council.

power the king desires to know of our faith, which is the one and true faith, he should send to his friends, while I should write to my brothers, so that there might come my fellow bishops, who, together with us, might succeed in explaining to you the faith we have in common, and in particular the Roman church, which is the head of all the churches."

44 To these words Obadus replied: "Are you therefore like my lord the king?" Bishop Eugenius said: "I am not like the king, but I said: If he wishes to know the true faith, let him write to his friends so that they may send our catholic bishops here, and let me write[26] to my fellow bishops, because it is the common concern of the catholic, universal church." Eugenius acted in this way, not because people capable of refuting the charges of our enemies were lacking in Africa, but so that there would come people who, being foreigners, would have greater assurance of being free from their power, and by the same token would make known to all lands and peoples the false basis on which we are oppressed.

45 But the one who was weaving plots did not wish to listen to reason. Acting frequently on pretexts, he troubled those bishops whom he had heard were learned with various hardships. Already he had sent into exile Secundianus of Mimiana[27], having subjected him to 150 blows with clubs, as well as Praesidius of Sufetula (Sbeitla), a very clear-sighted man. Then he had the venerable Mansuetus, Germanus, Fusculus and many others set upon with cudgels.

46 While these things were going on he ordered that no-one was to share a table with those of our religion; in fact, in no circumstances were people to eat with Catholics. This conferred no benefit on them, but was of the greatest advantage to us. For if 'their speech,' as the apostle says, 'is accustomed to crawl like a crab' (cf II Tim 2:17), how much more would sharing a table of food be able to bring defilement, since the same apostle says 'do not share food with the wicked.' (cf I Cor 5:11)

---

[26] 'Scribo', although the subjunctive or future would make more sense.

[27] On the form of this place name, consult Mandouze 1982:1049.

47 But when the fire of persecution was already kindled and the flame
of the attacking king burned everywhere, our God displayed through
his servant Eugenius a miracle which I must not pass over. In that same
town of Carthage there was a certain blind man, a citizen very well
known in the town, whose name was Felix. This man was visited by the
Lord and was told by him in a vision one night, when the day of the
Epiphany was dawning, "Rise, go to my servant bishop Eugenius, and
tell him that I have sent you to him. And at the time when he blesses
the font so that those coming to the faith may be baptized, he will
touch your eyes. They will be opened and you will see the light."[28]

48 Having been instructed by this vision, the blind man believed that
he had been deluded by a dream, as often happens, and decided not to
get up. But while he was sinking back to sleep, he was urged in the
same fashion to go to Eugenius. Again he paid no attention, and a
third time he was threatened, speedily and fiercely. He roused the boy
who usually guided him by the hand, and went with all speed to the
basilica of Faustus. When he came there he prayed with many tears
and asked a deacon, Peregrinus by name, to announce his arrival to the
bishop, indicating that he had a secret of some kind to make known to
him.

49 Hearing of this the bishop ordered the man to come in. Because of
the feast day that was being celebrated, the hymns of the night were
already resounding throughout the church as the people sang. The
blind man told the bishop the story of his vision and said to him: "I will
not let you go until you let me have my sight back, just as you have
been ordered by the Lord." The holy Eugenius said to him: "Depart
from me, brother, for I am an unworthy sinner (cf Luke 5:8) and a
wrongdoer above all men, seeing that even in these times I have been
preserved."

50 But that man held onto his knees and said nothing beyond what he
had said earlier: "Restore my sight to me, as has been ordered."

---

[28] Another miracle story involving Eugenius and a blind man, or perhaps another version
of the same story, is told by Gregory of Tours, *hist franc* 2.3.

Eugenius paid attention to his reverent trust and, because time was now pressing, he proceeded with him to the font in the company of the officiating clergy. There, immovable on his knees and groaning deeply, he disturbed heaven with his sobs. He blessed the rippling baptismal pool,[29] and when he had completed his prayer he arose and replied to the blind man in this way: "I have already told you, Felix my brother, that I am a sinful man; but may he who has deigned to visit you act in accordance with your faith and open your eyes." At the same time he signed his eyes with the standard of the cross, and immediately the blind man received his sight, as the Lord gave it back. The bishop kept him with him until all had been baptized in case the crowd, excited by such a great miracle, should crush the man who had received the light.

51 Afterwards the miracle was made public throughout the church. The man who had been blind went forward to the altar with Eugenius to return to the Lord a thank offering for the restoration of his health, in accordance with the custom. The bishop received it and placed it on the altar. In the joy that followed, an uproar which could not be controlled arose from the people. Immediately, a messenger went to the tyrant. Felix was seized, and he was asked what had happened and how he had received the light. He explained everything in proper order, and the bishops of the Arians said: "Eugenius did this through sorcery." Overwhelmed with confusion, they could not obscure the light, because Felix was a public figure well known to the whole city; nevertheless, they would have killed him, if it had been right, just as the Jews desired to put Lazarus to death after he had been raised from the dead.[30]

52 That day of treachery which the king had appointed, 1 February, was now drawing near. There came together not only the bishops of the whole of Africa, but also those of many of the islands, worn out with

---

[29] 'crispantem benedixit alveum fontis', which I take to refer to the rippling surface of a body of water large enough for adult candidates for baptism to be immersed in. See the photo of a lovely sixth century African font in Browning 1971: 131.

[30] An apparent misreading of John 11: 45-53.

suffering and grief.[31] Silence was observed for many days, until he separated every skilled and learned man from among them, so that they could be put to death on the basis of false charges. For he committed to the flames one of that choir of the learned, whose name was Laetus, a vigorous and most learned man, after he had long endured a squalid imprisonment.[32] He thought that making an example of him would strike fear into the others and enable him to wear them down.

53 Finally the debate took place, needless to say at a place their enemies had selected. Our people chose to avoid the disturbances which loud voices would have caused, in case the Arians were later to say that they had been overpowered by weight of numbers, and chose ten of their number who would answer on behalf of them all. Cyrila, with his lackeys, most arrogantly placed a throne for himself in a high place, while our people were standing. And our bishops said: "It is always pleasant to be at a meeting at which the exaltation of power does not proudly hold sway, but general consent is arrived at, so that the truth is recognized from what the judges decree, in accordance with the actions of the parties. But who is to be the judge on this occasion, who will weigh the evidence so that the scales of justice may confirm what has been argued well or show unsound propositions to be false?"[33]

54 While these and other things were being said, the king's notary answered: "The patriarch Cyrila has named some people." Our people, abominating the proud and unlawful title which he had usurped, said: "Read out to us who gave permission for Cyrila to take this title for

---

[31] The bishops are named in the *Notitia provinciarum civitatum Africae*, which is known from one ninth century ms and a lost ms whose readings are preserved in a book of the sixteenth century, and edited by Halm and Petschenig in their editions of Victor. The document is discussed by Courtois 1954: 91-100.

[32] The martyrdom of Laetus was known to Victor of Tunnunna (*chron s.a.* 479, 534, followed by Isidore of Seville *hist vand* 83).

[33] The Catholics seem to have feared that Cyrila, seated, would be their judge. It is instructive to compare with this account the importance attached to body language by the participants in the conference of Carthage in 411 (Brown 1967: 332ff).

himself!"[34] At this our enemies made a loud clamour and began to
bring false accusations. And because our people had sought that, if the
throng of sensible people were not allowed to ask questions, they could
at least look on, the order was given that all the children of the
catholic church who were present were to be beaten with a hundred
blows each. Then blessed Eugenius began to cry out: "May God see the
violence we endure, let him know the affliction we suffer from the
persecutors!"

55 Our people turned round and said to Cyrila: "Say what you intend
to do." Cyrila said: "I do not know Latin." Our bishops said: "We know
very well that you have always spoken Latin; you should not excuse
yourself now, especially since you have set this fire going."[35] And,
seeing that the catholic bishops were better prepared for the debate, he
flatly refused to give them a hearing, relying on various quibbles. But
our people had foreseen this and written a short work concerning the
faith, composed quite fittingly and with the necessary detail. They said:
"If you wish to know our faith, this is the truth we hold."[36]

THE BOOK OF THE CATHOLIC FAITH

56 We are enjoined by a royal command to provide an account of the
catholic faith which we hold. So we are setting out to indicate briefly
the things which we believe and proclaim, aware of our lack of ability
but supported by divine assistance. We recognize, then, that the first
thing we must do is give an explanation of the unity of the substance
of the Father and the Son, which the Greeks call *homousion*.

---

[34] Gregory of Tours was not even prepared to concede to Cyrila the title of bishop, but
termed him a priest (*hist franc* 2.3).

[35] In view of the progress of Latin among the Vandals and other barbarian peoples,
Cyrila's claim that he did not know Latin can hardly be taken seriously.

[36] Gennadius asserts that Eugenius composed an exposition of the catholic faith which it
is tempting to identify with the following document. But Eugenius' name is not among those
given at 2.101. An interesting letter of Eugenius to the Catholics of Carthage is preserved by
Gregory of Tours, *hist franc* 2.3, but its contents are quite different to those of the *Book of the
catholic faith*.

Therefore: we acknowledge the Father, the Son and the Holy Spirit in the unity of the divine nature in such a way that we can say with a faithful confession that the Father subsists as a distinct person, and the Son equally exists in his own person, and that the Holy Spirit retains the distinctiveness of his own person, not asserting that the Father is the same as the Son, nor confessing that the Son is the same as the Father or the Holy Spirit, nor understanding the Holy Spirit in such a way that he is the Father or the Son; but we believe the unbegotten Father and the Son begotten of the Father and the Holy Spirit proceeding from the Father[37] to be of one substance and essence, because the unbegotten Father and the begotten Son and the Holy Spirit who proceeds have one divine nature in common; nevertheless, there are three distinct persons.

57 A heresy arose and brought forth something new against this catholic and apostolic faith. It maintained that the Son was not born of the substance of the Father but came into being from no existing things, that is, out of nothing. To refute and completely destroy this wicked profession which had come forth against the faith, a Greek word, *homousion*, was coined. This means 'of one substance and essence,' and signifies that the Son was not born from no existing things nor from any substance, but of the Father. Therefore, whoever thinks that the word *homousion* is to be laid aside wishes to assert that the Son came to exist out of nothing. But if the Son is not 'of nothing,' he is without doubt of the Father, and rightly *homousion*, that is, of one substance with the Father.

58 That he is of the Father, that is, of one substance with the Father, is demonstrated by these testimonies. The apostle says: 'who, while he is the brightness of his glory and the figure of his substance, also upholds all things by the word of his power.' (Heb 1:3) And again God the Father himself, reproving the bad faith of the unbelievers who did not wish to hear the voice, abiding in his substance, of the Son who spoke through the prophets, said: 'They have not heard the voice of my

---

[37] The Spirit is seen as proceeding from the Father, but not from the Father and the Son (filioque), the position adopted in later western theology; so too below at 2.95.

substance.' (cf Jer 9:10 Vulg) And when the voice of his substance was despised, he rebuked them with a terrifying declaration, speaking to the same prophet and saying: 'Take up a lament on the mountains and a dirge on the paths of the desert, because they are in want, for they are not men. They have not heard the voice of my substance, from the birds of heaven to the herd.' (cf Jer 9:10 Vulg) And again he rebuked those who, falling away from the acknowledgement of one substance, did not wish to stand firm in the same substance of faith, saying: 'If they had stood firm in my substance and given heed to my words I would certainly have directed them from their evil path and from their wicked thoughts.' (cf Jer 23:22) And again he declares in a most open way that the Son is to be confessed as not foreign to the substance of the Father, but to be considered faithfully in the mind's eye as being in the same substance, when the prophet says: 'Who has stood firm in the substance of the Lord and heard his word?' (cf Jer 23:18)

59 Therefore, that the Son is the substance of the Father was formerly indicated by the prophetic oracles. As Solomon says, 'for you showed your substance and your sweetness, which is yours in the Son' (cf Wisd 16:21); this, in the figure and image of heavenly bread, was seen to pour out of heaven for the people of Israel. The Lord himself explained this in the Gospel, saying 'Moses did not give you bread from heaven, but my Father gives you bread from heaven' (Joh 6:32), and he indicates most surely that he was the bread when he says 'I am the living bread which has come down from heaven' (Joh 6:51), concerning which the prophet David also speaks: 'Man has eaten the bread of angels.' (Ps 77:25)

60 For indeed, so that the unity of substance which the Father and the Son have and their equal divinity might be shown still more evidently, he himself says in the Gospel 'I am in the Father and the Father is in me' (Joh 14:10), and 'I and the Father are one.' (Joh 10:30) This does not merely pertain to a unity of will, but to one and the same substance, because he did not say 'I and the Father have one will', but 'are one.' And so his unity with the Father is made clear not so much from what they will as from what they are. Again, John the evangelist says: 'For this reason the Jews sought to kill him, because not only did he break the Sabbath but he called God his Father, making himself

equal to God.' (Joh 5:18) Now this opinion is not at all to be ascribed to the Jews, because the evangelist truthfully said of the Son that he represented himself as equal to God.

61 Again, in the same Gospel it is written: 'Whatever the Father does, similarly the Son does the same things.' (Joh 5:19) And: 'Just as the Father raises the dead and gives them life, so the Son as well gives life to those he wishes.' (Joh 5:21) Again: 'That all may honour the Son, just as they honour the Father' (Joh 5:23), for equal honour is only shown to equals. Again, where the Son says to the Father: 'All things that are mine are yours, and all things that are yours are mine.' (Joh 17:10) Again: 'Philip, he who has seen me has seen the Father as well. How then can you say "Show us the Father."?' (Joh 14:9) He would not have said this if he had not been equal to the Father in all respects. Again, the Lord himself says: 'You believe in God; believe also in me.' (Joh 14:1)

62 Moreover, to show the unity and the equality, he says: 'No-one knows the Son except the Father, nor does anyone know the Father except the Son and anyone to whom the Son wishes to reveal him.' (Matt 11:27) And just as the Son reveals the Father to whom he wishes, so too the Father reveals the Son, just as he himself said to Peter when he confessed that he was the Christ, the Son of the living God: 'Blessed are you, Simon Bar-Jonah, because flesh and blood have not revealed this to you, but my Father who is in heaven.' (Matt 16:17) And again the Son says: 'No-one comes to the Father, but by me.' (Joh 14:6) And: 'No-one comes to me unless the Father who sent me leads him.' (Joh 6:44) The equality of the Father and the Son is clear from this, since they bring believers to themselves reciprocally. Again he says: 'If you had known me you would certainly have known my Father as well; from now on you know him and have seen him.' (Joh 14:7)

63 But since we acknowledge two natures in the Son, he being true God and true man, having a body and a soul, we feel that whatever excellent and sublime power the scriptures speak of as being his should be ascribed to his wonderful divinity, while whatever is said of the same person in a more lowly fashion and is beneath the dignity of heavenly power we take to refer not to God the word but to the humanity he

assumed. Therefore, it was with regard to his divinity that he spoke in the words we quoted earlier: 'I and the Father are one', and 'He who has seen me has seen the Father as well', and 'Whatever the Father does, in a similar manner the Son does the same things,' as well as the other passages contained above.

64 But those passages which speak of him with regard to his humanity are as follows: 'The Father is greater than I' (Joh 14:28), and 'I have come not to do my will, but the will of him who sent me' (Joh 6:38), and 'Father, if it can be done, let this cup pass from me' (Matt 26:39); also when he says from the cross 'God, my God, why have you forsaken me?' (Matt 27:46) And again, when the prophet speaks in the person of the Son: 'You are my God from the womb of my mother' (Ps 21:11), or when he is described as 'less than the angels' (Heb 2:7, cf Ps 8:6), and many passages like these which, for the sake of brevity, we have not included.

65 Therefore, the Son of God was constrained by no necessary circumstances, but it was by the unhampered power of his divinity that in his wonderful goodness he took upon himself those things which are ours in such a manner that he in no way set aside those things which are divine, because divinity can neither be added to nor suffer loss. Whence we thank our Lord Jesus Christ, who for us and for our salvation came down from heaven[38] and redeemed us by his passion, gave us life by his death, and glorified us by his ascension; who, seated at the right hand of the Father, will come to judge the living and the dead, to give to the just the reward of eternal life, but to render to the wrongdoers and unbelievers the punishments they deserve.

66 Therefore, we acknowledge that the Father has everlastingly begotten the Son from himself in an indescribable way, that is, from what he himself is, and that he was born not from an extraneous source, not from nothing, and not from some underlying material, but from God. And he who is born of God is nothing other than what the

---

[38] A form of words similar to a passage in the Nicene-Constantinopolitan creed; other examples of borrowing occur below at 2.70 and 2.74.

Father is, and on that account of one substance with him, because the reality of his birth does not permit a difference in kind. For if he is of another substance than the Father, he is either not a true son or, something dreadful to say, he was born degenerate.[39] For he is a true son, just as John says: 'that we be in his true son.' (I Joh 5:20 Vulg)

67 But he is not degenerate, because he was born true God of true God, just as the same John the evangelist goes on to say: 'This is the true God and eternal life.' (I Joh 5:20) And the Lord himself says in the Gospel: 'I am the way, the truth and the life.' (Joh 14:6) Therefore, if he does not derive his substance from another source, he takes it from the Father; if he takes it from the Father, he is of one substance with the Father. But if he is not of one substance, he is therefore not of the Father, but comes from another source, since it is necessary that he derive his substance from whence he comes: for all things were created from nothing, but the Son is of the Father. Each person may choose from the alternatives as he pleases: let him credit him with the substance of the Father, or let him confess that he came to exist out of nothing.

68 But perhaps someone will make an objection based on the words of the prophet: 'who shall tell his begetting?' (Is 53:8) But I did not say: "Tell me the means and manner of the divine begetting, and disclose in human words the secret of such a great mystery", since I was seeking to know from whence he was born, not in what manner he was born. The divine begetting is indescribable, but not incapable of being known. For it is not incapable of being known to this extent, namely, it is not unknown from whence he is, as very often the Father bears witness that he begat him from his very self and the Son bears witness that he was born of the Father, something as to which no Christian can have the slightest doubt, just as it is shown in the Gospel, when the Son himself says: 'For the person who does not believe has already been judged, because he does not believe in the name of the only begotten son of God.' (Joh 3:18) Again, John the evangelist says: 'And so we

---

[39] 'Degener', although the word means more than 'degenerate': if Christ were 'degener' he would not have been begotten (genitus) of the Father but different in kind (genus).

saw his glory, glory as of the only-begotten of the Father.' (Joh 1:14)
Therefore, we bring our profession of faith to an end with[40] a short
word.

69 If he was truly born of the Father, he is of one substance with him
and a true son; but if he is not of one substance and is not a true son,
he is not true God. Or, if he is true God and nevertheless is not of the
substance of the Father, it follows that he himself is unbegotten as well.
But because he is not unbegotten he is therefore a creature and, one
would think, if he is not of the substance of the Father, he takes his
existence from another source. But may no-one believe such a thing!
For we acknowledge the Son to be of one substance with the Father,
holding in detestation the Sabellian heresy which makes the Trinity so
indistinct as to say that the Father is the same as the Son and to
believe that the Holy Spirit is the same, not preserving the three
persons in the unity.

70 But perhaps someone will make an objection: given that the Father
is unbegotten and the Son begotten, it cannot be the case that the one
who is unbegotten and the one who is begotten have one and the same
substance. If the Son were unbegotten, just as the Father is, then to be
sure they would not have the same substance, because each of them,
coming to exist independently, would not have a substance in common
with the other. But since the unbegotten Father begat the Son of
himself, that is, of that which he himself is, if indeed what this is can
be said, since the manner of his coming to be cannot be spoken of at
all, it is clear that the begetter and the begotten have one substance,
because we truthfully acknowledge the Son to be 'God from God and
light from light.'[41]

71 For the apostle John bears witness that the Father is a light, saying:
'God is a light and there is no darkness in him.' (I Joh 1:5) Again, he
says of the Son: 'and the life was a light for people, and a light which

---

[40] Or perhaps 'we limit our profession of faith to'.

[41] At the price of some awkwardness, I have sought to express the argument of this
passage by translating where possible 'lux' as 'a light' and 'lumen' as 'the light'.

shone in the darkness, and the darkness has not overcome it.' (Joh
1:4f) And later on: 'He was the true light which shines on every person
who comes into this world.' (Joh 1:9 Vulg) From this it is clear that the
Father and the Son are of one substance, since the substances of a light
and the light, namely that which produces from itself and that which is
derived from that which produces, cannot be different. Finally, in case
anyone introduces a diversity of natural light between the Father and
the Son, the apostle speaks of the same Son in this way: 'while he is the
brightness of his glory and the figure of his substance.' (Heb 1:3 Vulg)
Here it is taught quite clearly that he is co-eternal with the Father,
inseparable from the Father and of one substance with him, since
brightness is always co-eternal with a light, since brightness is never
separated from the light, and since brightness can never be different to
a light in nature or substance. For the one who is the brightness of a
light is also the strength of God the Father, and so everlasting because
of the eternity of his strength, inseparable because of the unity of the
splendour.[42]

72 And this is what we faithfully acknowledge, the Son born of the
substance of the Father, just as God the Father himself makes clear in
a straightforward piece of evidence. To show that he had begotten his
own Son of the substance of his indescribable nature, for the purpose
of instructing our frailty and ignorance, to raise us up from things
visible to those invisible, he used a word which refers to earthly birth
to represent the case of the divine begetting, saying: 'I have begotten
you from the womb before dawn.' (Ps 109:3 Vulg) How could the
divinity have deigned to speak more clearly or more revealingly? What
signs, what examples from the things which exist could he have used to
indicate the nature of the begetting more effectively than indicating this
through the use of the word 'womb'? Not because he is composed of
bodily limbs or endowed with any lineaments and joints, but because
in the recesses of our mind we would not otherwise be able to
understand the truth of the divine begetting if we were not led on by
a term which applies to humans, 'womb.' So there can no longer be any

---

[42] 'Sempiternus ergo propter virtutis aeternitatem, inseperabilis propter claritudinis
unitatem', with which compare Ambrose de fide 4.9.108: 'coaeternus propter virtutis
aeternitatem, inseperabilis propter claritudinis unitatem'.

doubt that he who is agreed to have come forth from the womb of the Father was born of the substance of God.

73 Believing, therefore, that God the Father begat the Son from his own substance without suffering, we do not say that the substance was divided in the Son or underwent any diminution in the Father, and so could have been subject to the imperfection implied by suffering.[43] Far be it from us to think or imagine such things of God, because we faithfully acknowledge that the perfect Father begat the perfect Son without any diminution of himself, without any lessening and without the slightest weakness which suffering would have implied. For anyone who reproaches God that, if he begat from himself, he was subject to the imperfection of being divided, can just as well say that he found the work hard when he created all things, and that he rested from all his work on the seventh day for this reason. But he did not experience any suffering or diminution in begetting from himself; nor was he subject to any tiredness in creating all things.

74 For in order that the freedom from suffering in the divine begetting might be made known to us more clearly, we accept that the Son is to be acknowledged as God from God and light from light. If, therefore, when the visible light of this world is produced, it is not found that, when light was derived from light and arose from a kind of birth of begetting, the original light, having produced another light from itself, was diminished, and was not entirely capable of sustaining the loss of the light furnished out of itself, how much more rightly and fittingly is this to be believed of the nature of the divine light which is beyond description and which can in no way be diminished as it begets light out of itself? Whence the Son, not born in time but coeternal with the one who begets, is equal to the Father, just as the brightness begotten of a fire obviously lasts as long as the fire does. May it suffice to have said these things concerning the equality of the Father and the Son and of the unity of their substance, within the bounds which our desire for brevity has permitted.

---

[43]   I translate 'passio' as 'suffering.'

75 It remains for us to speak of the Holy Spirit, whom we believe consubstantial, co-equal and co-eternal with the Father and the Son, and to prove that he is this with pieces of evidence. For even though this Trinity, worthy of reverence, is distinct with reference to persons and names, nevertheless, it should not be believed that it differs from itself and from its eternity for this reason. Rather, it should be truly and properly believed that divinity has abided from before time in the Father and the Son and the Holy Spirit, and that this Trinity can neither be divided by interpretations of ours nor, in the opposite direction, can it be combined and turned into one person. This is our full faith; this is what we believe.

76 Hence we do not suffer them to be thought of as gods, or called this, but in the aforesaid persons and names we acknowledge one God. For the divinity, which is beyond description, did not reveal itself by means of names and persons so that it can be fenced in and laid hold of by words: but so that what it was might be known, it gave believers a partial understanding of itself, which would not be beyond the limitations of the human mind, in accordance with the words of the prophet: 'unless you believe you will not understand.' (cf Is 7:9) There is, therefore, one divine nature in the Trinity, and the use of this term in describing it signifies one substance, but not one person. To establish the truth of this for the faithful the divinity has always provided many and very frequent proofs in testimony of itself. We may be allowed, therefore, in the interests of brevity, to bring forward a few things from among many, for in truth, there is no need for a large number of testimonies to demonstrate majesty, even though these may exist, since for a believer a few things are enough.

77 Firstly, then, we shall teach that the Father, the Son and the Holy Spirit are of one substance from the books of the Old Testament, and afterwards those of the New as well. The book of Genesis begins in this way: 'In the beginning God made heaven and earth, but the earth was void[44] and without form, and darkness covered the abyss; and the

---

[44] 'Invisibilis', whereas the Vulgate has 'inanis'. For the use of 'invisibilis' in this sense, *TLL* 7: 220.20ff.

Spirit of God was borne above the waters.' (Gen 1:1f) The 'beginning'
is the one who said to the Jews when they asked who he was: 'I who
speak to you am the beginning.' (Joh 8:25 Vulg) The Spirit of God was
borne above the waters in his role as creator,[45] sustaining what had
been created by the strength of his power, so that from these waters he
could accomplish the bringing forth of all living things as he applied
the warmth of his own fire to the rough elements, and so that the
nature of the liquid, with the mystery of baptism shining forth even
then, might receive the power of his sanctification and bring to life the
first living bodies. In like manner David, inspired by God, bears
witness: 'The heavens were made fast by the word of the Lord, and all
their strength by the Spirit of his mouth.' (Ps 32:6)

78 See how full this brevity is, and how clearly it refers to the mystery
of the unity. Calling the Father 'Lord' and signifying the Son by 'word,'
it designates the Holy Spirit the 'mouth of the highest' (Sir 24:5). In
case 'word' is taken to refer to something produced by a voice, he
asserts that the heavens were made fast through him. And in case
'spirit' is thought to refer to breath,[46] he shows that the fullness of
heavenly strength is in him. For where there is strength it is necessary
that a person exists, and where he says 'all' he signifies a strength not
taken from the Father and the Son, but made perfect in the Holy
Spirit, so that he does not possess all by himself what is in the Father
and the Son, but so that he possesses in full whatever either of them
has.

79 And again, when the Lord spoke concerning the calling of the
nations, he proclaimed that the Holy Spirit is included within the one
name of the divinity when he says: 'Go forth and teach all nations,
baptizing them in the name of the Father and of the Son and of the
Holy Spirit.' (Matt 28:19) And again, when the apostle preached to the
Corinthians concerning heavenly things, he added these words: 'The
grace of our Lord Jesus Christ and the love of God and the fellowship

---

[45] The fathers frequently identify the 'spiritus Dei' of Gen 1:2 with the Holy Spirit; see
among many Augustine *conf* 13.4.5.

[46] 'Spiritus' can mean breath as well as spirit.

of the Holy Spirit be with you all.' (II Cor 13:14) And so that we may acknowledge more positively the unity of substance in this Trinity, we should consider as well how God, when he was attending to the creation of the world and of man, made the mystery of the Trinity known, when he said 'Let us make man in our image and likeness.' (Gen 1:26) By saying 'our' he assuredly shows that it was not the affair of just one person, but when he mentions 'image and likeness' he indicates that the persons who are differentiated are equal. And so that the same work may contain an open reference to the Trinity in which plurality is not wanting, and the likeness is not dissimilar, the following passages say: 'and God spoke and God acted and God blessed.' (Gen 1:3,7,28 etc) And it is necessary that one God be the author of the entire creation.

80   Finally, the old blessing given through Moses, which he was ordered to use in blessing the people with a mystery of threefold invocation, expands and confirms this system of faith. For God said to Moses: 'Thus you shall bless my people. and I shall bless them: May the Lord bless you and keep you; may the Lord make his face to shine upon you and be merciful to you; may the Lord lift up his countenance upon you and give you peace.' (cf Num 6:23-26) The prophet David confirms this very thing, when he says 'May God bless us, our God, may God bless us and may all the ends of the earth fear him.' (Ps 66:7f) This is the unity of the Trinity which the angelic powers on high venerate in their hymn, and, in the threefold 'holy, holy, holy Lord God of hosts' (Is 6:3) which they sing with unresting lips, they exult his glory in the summit of one dominion.

81 So that this may be impressed on the understanding of the faithful still more clearly, we bring forward Paul, a person with knowledge of heavenly mysteries. For he says: 'There are different gifts, but the same Spirit; and different ministries, but the same Lord; and different workings, but the same God who works all in all.' (I Cor 12:4-6) It is certain that, when he distinguished between the various charisms, he taught that the Holy Spirit brings about these differences and divisions in accordance with the quality and merit of those who share in them, for he concludes by saying: 'But one and the same Spirit works all

these things, distributing of his own to each one, just as he wills.' (I Cor 12:11)

82 And so, no occasion for uncertainty is left. It is clear that the Holy Spirit is also God and the author of his own will, he who is most clearly shown to be at work in all things and to bestow the gifts of the divine dispensation according to the judgment of his own will, because where it is proclaimed that he distributes graces where he wills, servile condition cannot exist, for servitude is to be understood in what is created, but power and freedom in the Trinity. And so that we may teach the Holy Spirit to be of one divinity with the Father and the Son still more clearly than the light, here is proof from the testimony of John the evangelist. For he says: 'There are three who bear witness in heaven, the Father, the Word and the Holy Spirit, and these three are one.'[47] Surely he does he not say 'three separated by a difference in quality' or 'divided by grades which differentiate, so that there is a great distance between them?' No, he says that the 'three are one.'

83 But so that the single divinity which the Holy Spirit has with the Father and the Son might be demonstrated still more in the creation of all things, you have in the book of Job the Holy Spirit as a creator: 'It is the divine Spirit who made me, and the Spirit of the almighty who teaches me.' (cf. Job 33:4) And David says: 'Send forth your Spirit and they will be created, and you shall renew the face of the earth.' (Ps 103:30) If creation and renewal will take place through the Spirit, without doubt the beginning of the creation as well was not carried out without the Spirit. Let us therefore show that after the creation the Spirit gives life, just as the Father and the Son do. Now, the apostle relates concerning the person of the Father: 'I am a witness in the sight of God, who gives life to all things.' (cf I Tim 6:13) But Christ gives life: 'My sheep,' he says, 'hear my voice, and I give them eternal life.' (Joh 10:27f) But we are given life by the Holy Spirit, as the Lord himself says: 'It is the Spirit who gives life.' (Joh 6:64) Behold, it is

---

[47] The famous Johannine comma, occurring in the text of I Joh at 5:8, but certainly not a part of the original text. The circumstances of its addition remain obscure.

plainly shown that there is one giving of life common to the Father, the Son and the Holy Spirit.

84 No Christian can be unaware that foreknowledge of all things and knowledge of what is hidden belong to God. Nevertheless, this can be shown from the book of Daniel: 'God,' he says, 'you know what is hidden, you who have foreknowledge of all people before they are born.' (Dan 13:42 Vulg) This same foreknowledge is a property of Christ, just as the evangelist relates: 'From the beginning Jesus knew who would betray him, and who those who did not believe in him were.' (cf Joh 6:65) That he knew things which were hidden is clear from what he said when making public the hidden counsels of the Jews: 'Why do you think evil in your hearts?' (Matt 9:4)

85 He himself made it clear that the Holy Spirit, in a similar fashion, has foreknowledge of all things, when he said to the apostles: 'When the Spirit of truth comes he will teach you all things and make known to you things which are to come.' (Joh 16:13) There can be no doubt that one who is said to make known things which are to come has foreknowledge of all things, because he himself probes the depths of God and knows all that is in God, just as Paul relates when he says: 'the Spirit probes all things, even the depths of God.' (I Cor 2:10) Again, in the same place: 'Just as no man knows what belongs to man, except the spirit which is in him, so no-one knows what belongs to God, except the Spirit of God.' (I Cor 2:11)

86 But in order that the mightiness of the Holy Spirit may be understood, we shall mention a few things which are among the awe-inspiring. A deceitful disciple had sold his property, as is written in the Acts of the Apostles, but kept back part of the money and laid down what was left at the feet of the apostles, as if it were the whole. He offended the Holy Spirit, from whom he thought he could hide. But what did the blessed Peter say to him straightaway? 'Annanias, why has Satan filled your heart, so that you have lied to the Holy Spirit?' (Acts 5:3) And further on: 'You have lied not to men, but to God.' (Acts 5:4) So it was that he was struck down by the power of the one to whom he had been willing to lie and breathed his last. And how does blessed Peter wish the Holy Spirit to be understood in this place? It is very

clear, when he says "You have lied not to men, but to God." It is
therefore obvious that, since one who lies to the Holy Spirit lies to
God, one who believes in the Holy Spirit believes in God.

87 Of the same kind, but more powerful, is what the Lord discloses in
the Gospel when he says: 'Every sin and blasphemy shall be forgiven
men, but he who blasphemes against the Holy Spirit shall not be
forgiven in this age or the age to come.' (Matt 12:31f) Behold the
terrifying decree: he says that one who blasphemes against the Holy
Spirit commits a sin which cannot be forgiven. Compare with this
decree what is written in the book of Kings: 'If a man sins by sinning
against a man they shall pray for him, but if he sins against God, who
shall pray for him?' (cf I Sam 2:25) Therefore, since blaspheming
against the Holy Spirit and sinning against God are similar, in that the
offence cannot be atoned for, everyone can now understand how great
the Holy Spirit is.

88 That God is present everywhere and fills all things we learn from
the mouth of Isaiah: 'I, says God, am near, and not far off. Therefore,
if a man conceals himself in hiding places, shall I not see him? Do I
not fill heaven and earth?' (cf Jer 23:23f) And what does the Saviour
say in the Gospel concerning his presence everywhere? 'Wherever two
or three are gathered together in my name, there am I in the midst of
them.' (Matt 18:20) Speaking in the person of God, the prophet
indicates that the Holy Spirit, equally, is everywhere: 'I am in you and
my Spirit stands in your midst.' (cf Ez 36:27) And Solomon says: 'The
Spirit of the Lord fills the wide earth and that which holds all things
together knows his voice.' (Wisd 1:7) Again, David says: 'Where shall
I go from your Spirit, and where shall I flee from your face? If I go up
to heaven, you are there; if I go down to hell, you are present; if I take
my wings in a straight line and live by the furthest part of the sea, you
shall lead me there, and your right hand shall sustain me.' (Ps 138:7-9)

89 God dwells in his saints, according to the promise in which he said:
'I shall dwell in them.' (II Cor 6:16) And what the Lord Jesus says in
the Gospel, 'Remain in me and I in you,' (Joh 15:4) is assented to by
Paul when he says 'Do you not know that Jesus Christ is in you?' (II
Cor 13;5) All this is fulfilled in the dwelling of the Spirit, just as John

mentions: 'From this,' he says, 'we know that he is in us, because he has given to us of his Spirit.' (cf I Joh 4:13) In the same vein is Paul as well: 'Do you not know that you are the temple of God and that the Spirit of God dwells in you?' (I Cor 3:16) And again, he says: 'Glorify God and carry him about in your body.' (I Cor 6:20 Vulg) Which God? To be sure, the Holy Spirit, whose temple, as we have seen, we are.

90 That the Son and the Holy Spirit rebuke that which the Father rebukes can be proved in this way. In psalm 49 we read: 'God says to the sinner' and, further on, 'I rebuke you and issue a decree before your face.' (Ps 49:16,21) In the same way David, at prayer, speaks to Christ: 'Lord, do not rebuke me in your wrath,' (Ps 6:2) because he was to come to rebuke all flesh. But what does the Saviour say in the Gospel concerning the Holy Spirit? 'When the Paraclete comes,' he says, 'he will rebuke the world concerning sin, righteousness and judgment.' (Joh 16:8) Foreseeing this, David cried out to the Lord 'Where shall I go from your Spirit, and where shall I flee from your face?' (Ps 138:7)

91 That the Father is good, the Son is good and the Holy Spirit is good can be proved as follows. The prophet says: 'You are good, Lord; of your goodness, teach me your precepts.' (Ps 118:68) But the only-begotten says of himself: 'I am the good shepherd.' (Joh 10:11) Equally, David speaks to God concerning the Holy Spirit in a psalm: 'Your good Spirit shall lead me in the right way.' (Ps 142:10)

92 But who could remain silent as to the dignity of the Holy Spirit? For of old the prophets cried out: 'Thus says the Lord.' (Ex 5:1 etc) When Christ came, he applied this expression to his own person when he said: 'But I say to you.' (Matt 5:22) And what did the new prophets cry out? Just as the prophet Agabus did in the Acts of the Apostles: 'Thus says the Holy Spirit.' (Acts 21:11) And Paul says to Timothy: 'The Spirit clearly says.' (I Tim 4:1) This expression makes the absence of distinction within the Trinity completely clear. And indeed, Paul says that he was called and sent by God the Father and by Christ: 'Paul,' he says, 'an apostle not from men or through man but through Jesus Christ and God the Father.' (Gal 1:1) In the Acts of the Apostles one reads that he was set apart and sent by the Holy Spirit. For it is

written: 'Thus says the Holy Spirit: "Set Barnabas and Saul apart for me for the work to which I have called them."' (Acts 13:2) And a little later it says: 'Sent by the Holy Spirit, they went down to Seleucia.' (Acts 13:4) Again, in the same book: 'Pay attention to yourselves and to the whole flock in which the Holy Spirit has appointed you bishops.' (Acts 20:28)

93   Let no-one consider that the Holy Spirit is in some way contemptible because he is called 'Paraclete', for a paraclete is an 'advocate', or rather 'comforter,' in the Latin language, and this is a title he shares with the Son of God, just as John teaches: 'These things,' he says, 'I write to you so that you do not sin, but if anyone sins we have a paraclete with the Father, Jesus Christ.'[48] For the Lord himself says to the apostles: 'the Father will send you another Paraclete' (Joh 14:16), and there can be no doubt that when he says 'another Paraclete' he indicates that he is a paraclete as well. And neither is the title 'paraclete' inappropriate to the Father, for it is a title applied to beneficence, not to nature.

94 Finally, Paul writes to the Corinthians in these terms: 'Blessed be the God and Father of our Lord Jesus Christ, the Father of mercies and the God of all comfort, who comforts us.' (II Cor 1:3f) And although the Father is called comforter, the Son is called comforter, and the Holy Spirit is called comforter as well, nevertheless there is one comfort provided to us by the Trinity, just as there is one remission of sins, as the apostle affirms: 'You have been washed,' he says, 'and justified, and you have been sanctified in the name of our Lord Jesus Christ and in the Spirit of our God.' (I Cor 6:11) We could have brought forth more testimonies from the divine scriptures which, in accordance with the sacrament of baptism,[49] disclose a Trinity of one glory, operation and power, but because the full understanding of these things is for the wise, we have passed over many things for the sake of brevity.

---

[48] cf I Joh 2:1, but whereas the Vulgate has 'advocatum', the text here reads 'paraclitum'.

[49] Presumably a reference to the formula for baptism given at Matt 28:19.

95 And so let us summarize what we have said. If the Holy Spirit proceeds from the Father, if he sets free, if he is the lord and sanctifies, if he creates together with the Father and the Son, if he gives life, if he has foreknowledge together with the Father and the Son, if he is everywhere and fills all things, if he lives in the elect, if he rebukes the world, if he judges, if he is good and upright, if it is proclaimed of him 'thus says the Holy Spirit' (Acts 21:11), if he appoints prophets, if he sends apostles, if he places bishops in authority, if he is the comforter, if he dispenses all things as he wills, if he washes and justifies, if he kills those who put him to the test, if one who blasphemes him will have remission neither in this age nor the one to come, something which is thoroughly appropriate to God: all this being the case, why do people doubt that he is God, since he reveals what he is by the greatness of his works? One who is not different to the Father and the Son in the strength of his works is certainly not different to them in majesty.

96 In vain do they deny the title 'divine' to one whose power they cannot refuse to acknowledge, in vain do they prohibit me from venerating with the Father and the Son him whom I am driven to acknowledge together with the Father and the Son. If he, together with the Father and the Son, bestows on me the remission of sins, and bestows sanctification and eternal life, it would be thoroughly ungrateful and wicked of me were I not to ascribe him glory with the Father and the Son. Or: if he should not be worshipped with the Father and the Son, he should therefore not be acknowledged in baptism. But if the words of the Lord and the tradition of the apostles make it quite clear that he is to be acknowledged, lest the faith be only half complete, who will prohibit me from worshipping him? For I shall also make due supplications to one in whom I am ordered to believe. Therefore, I shall adore the Father, I shall adore the Son, and I shall adore the Holy Spirit, with one and the same veneration.

97 Now if someone considers this hard, let him hear how David exhorts the faithful to the worship of God: 'Adore,' he says, 'his footstool.' (Ps 98:5 Vulg) If the adoration of his footstool is a characteristic of religion, how much more should his Spirit be adored? He is certainly that Spirit whom blessed Peter proclaimed with such

sublimity when he spoke of 'the Holy Spirit sent down from heaven, whom the angels long to catch sight of.' (cf I Pet 1:12) If the angels long to catch sight of him, how much more ought we mortals not look down on him, in case what was said to the Jews happens to be said to us as well: 'You have always resisted the Holy Spirit, just like your fathers.' (Acts 7:51)

98 But if these considerations, so great and of such kinds, do not incline the heart to venerate the Holy Spirit, pay attention to something still more powerful. For Paul instructed the prophets of the church, in whom and through whom the Holy Spirit spoke in particular, in this way: 'If,' he said, 'all prophesy, and some unbeliever or unlearned person comes in, he is convicted by all, put to the trial by all, the hidden things of his heart are revealed; and then, falling on his face, he will adore God and declare that God is truly in you.' (I Cor 14:24f) And the Holy Spirit who prophesies is obviously in these people. Therefore, if unbelievers fall on their faces and, terrified, adore the Holy Spirit and confess him against their will, how much more is it proper for the faithful to adore the Holy Spirit of their free will and out of love? But the Holy Spirit is not adored by himself, in the manner of the gentiles,[50] just as the Son is not adored by himself, because he is at the right hand of the Father; but when we adore the Father we believe that we adore the Son and the Holy Spirit, and when we invoke the Son we believe that we invoke the Father, and when we pray to the Father we believe that we are heard by the Son, just as the Lord himself said: 'Whatever you ask the Father in my name, I shall do, so that the Father might be honoured in the Son.' (Joh 14:13) And if the Holy Spirit is adored, the one whose spirit he is, is assuredly adored as well.

99 But there can be no-one ignorant of the fact that nothing can be added to or taken away from the divine majesty by human supplications, but each person, following the intention of his will, gains either glory by worshipping faithfully, or everlasting shame by resisting

---

[50] That is, the Spirit is not treated as a separate deity in a polytheistic manner. A similar point is made at 2.100.

stubbornly. For it is certain that strife and pride condemn, but that the fruit of devotion will be the bestowing of honour. Why should the faithful not give honour to the Trinity, to which they trust they belong, in its fullness? They take pride in having been born again in its name and in describing themselves as its servants. For just as men of God are called this with reference to the name of God the Father, so that Elijah was termed 'man of God' and Moses was called 'man of God,' so we Christians take our name from Christ, and so too we are called 'spiritual' after the Spirit. If, therefore, someone is called 'man of God' and is not a Christian, he is nothing; if someone is called 'Christian' and is not spiritual, he should not be too confident of his salvation.

100 Let us therefore have a full faith in the Trinity, in accordance with the profession of that baptism which brings salvation, and one devotion and piety, and let us not think, as do the gentiles, of different powers, or receive in the Trinity a created being when it is a question of the divine nature. But neither let us be troubled by something which causes offence to the Jews who deny the Son of God and do not adore the Holy Spirit; rather, adoring and magnifying the full Trinity, let us, just as we say with our mouth when celebrating the mysteries, also hold inwardly 'Holy, holy, holy Lord God of hosts.' (Is 6:3) Saying 'holy' three times we acknowledge one omnipotence, because there is one religion and one rendering of glory to the Trinity, as we can hear from the apostle just as the Corinthians heard it: 'The grace of our Lord Jesus Christ and the love of God and the fellowship of the Holy Spirit be with you all.' (II Cor 13:13)

101 This is our faith, confirmed by evangelical and apostolic traditions and authority, and founded on the association of all the catholic churches which are in this world; in which faith we trust and hope we shall remain, by the grace of almighty God, until the end of this life. Amen.

This is the end of the book sent on 20 April by Januarius of Zattara (Kef Benzioune) and Villaticus of Casae Medianae, bishops of Numidia, and Boniface of Foratiana and Boniface of Gratiana, bishops of Byzacena.

BOOK 3

1 When our little book had been presented to them and read out, their blind eyes found it impossible to endure the light of the truth. They raved with intolerable shouts, taking it amiss that in the title of the book we had called ourselves 'Catholics'.[1] Straightaway those liars declared to the king that we had created an uproar while rushing away from the hearing. He was immediately inflamed and, believing the falsehood, lost no time in doing what he wanted to do.

2 He had already drawn up a decree and secretly sent his men with it throughout the different provinces. So, while the bishops were in Carthage, in one day he closed the churches throughout Africa and he presented all the property of the bishops and churches to his own bishops as a gift. Also, 'without understanding what it said and the things it asserted'. (cf I Tim 1:7), they did not blush for shame in deploying against us a law which our Christian emperors, seeking to do honour to the catholic church, had previously issued against them and other heretics,[2] to which they added many things of their own, just as seemed good to their tyrannical power. This is the text of the law which was issued and published.

3 "Hunirix, king of the Vandals and Alans, to all the peoples subject to our sovereignty. It is well known that the casting back of evil counsels against those who give them is a feature of triumphant majesty and royal strength. For whoever devises something depraved must blame himself for what happens to him. In this matter our clemency has been guided by the will of the divine judgment, which deals with all people in accordance with what their deeds, whether they have been good or, as it may be, the reverse, have deserved: it makes some pay

---

[1] The reading of a document of this length would have been conducive to feelings of restlessness. Augustine observed that all heretics wished to be called Catholics: *con ep fund* 4.5 (*PL* 42:175).

[2] Imperial legislation against heretics is gathered in *cod theod* 16.5, where 16.5.6, 8, 11-13, 16, 59f and 65f mention Arians. Other sources which mention the following events are not detailed: *Laterculus reg VVand et Al (MGH AA* 13:458); Victor of Tunnunna *chron s.a.* 466, 479; Procopius *BV* 1.8.3f. As with the official documents reproduced by Victor in book 2, the Latin of this document is tortuous.

a penalty, while it turns out that others are rewarded. And so we have adopted a severe judgment against these provocative people who believe that what our father of glorious memory and our own mildness have commanded should be despised.

4   "For we had all the peoples notified of our orders that the homousian priests were to presume to hold no liturgies in the lands of the Vandals,[3] nor were they to take it upon themselves to celebrate the mysteries, things which in fact pollute. When we saw that this was disregarded, and many came to our attention who said that they kept the rule of faith in its entirety, it is well known that all were advised that a debate, to take place nine months later, had been allowed, in case some part of their opinion could be accommodated, and that they were to assemble without any fear on 25 February of the eighth year of our reign.

5   "When they came together here at the town of Carthage, after the prescribed time had passed, we granted, as is recognized, a further deferment of some days. And when they affirmed that they were prepared for the debate, it is well known that on the first day our venerable bishops proposed to them that they prove the homousion in a proper fashion from the divine Scriptures, just as they had been asked to, failing which they would certainly condemn something which was done away with by a thousand and more bishops from the whole world at the council of Ariminum and at Seleucia.[4]

6   "But they, using the people whom they had stirred up, brought everything into confusion, and showed not the slightest desire to do this. On the contrary, on the second day, when we asked them to give an answer concerning that same faith, just as had been proposed, they took it upon themselves, with consummate foolhardiness, to throw

---

[3] *Sortes Vandalorum*, for which see above 1.13 with note. Wolfram suggests (1979:4) that the *sortes Vandalorum* of the early period of Vandal settlement were referred to as the *Regnum Vandalorum et Alanorum* in the next generation, which is possible.

[4] The Arianizing councils of Ariminum (Rimini) and Seleucia had been summoned by the emperor Constantius in 359.

everything into confusion with seditious shouting, with the intention of bringing it about that the debate did not take place.

7 "Provoked by these people, we ordered that their churches were to be closed. As expressed in a written communication to them, the terms were that they were to be closed until such time as they chose to come to the debate which had been proposed. But, impelled by an obstinacy which their wicked purposes seem to have led them to embrace, they did not wish to do this. And so it is necessary and very just to twist around against them what is shown to be contained in those very laws which happen to have been promulgated by the emperors of various times who, with them, had been led into error.[5]

8 "The purport of these laws was that no church was to have been kept open, except by the priests of their superstition: other priests were not allowed either to conduct assemblies or hold meetings, nor to possess or construct churches in cities or even in the tiniest places; these were to be taken over and added to the possessions of the fisc. In addition, their patrimonies, which had pertained to the churches of their faith, were to have passed to their priests. Such people were not to have been given the liberty to stay in any places at all, but they were to be banished from all cities and places. Nor were they to have any means for baptizing at their disposal, in case they should happen to dispute concerning religion; and they were to have no freedom to ordain bishops or priests or other ranks of clergy. A severe punishment was set forth: both those who permitted themselves to receive such honours and those who ordained them were to be fined ten pounds of gold each. Furthermore, there was to be no opportunity or possibility for them to make any petition, and even if they deserved special treatment they were not to prevail. And if they persisted in this wicked behaviour, they were also to be driven from their own land and sent into exile under a suitable guard.

9 "The aforementioned emperors also raged against the laity in a similar fashion, because they were to lose completely their right to

---

[5] For what follows, there is a helpful commentary by Overbeck 1973:77-79.

bestow and bequeath, or to receive what was left to them by others, whether in the form of a bequest held for someone else, or of a legacy, or of donations, or by that means termed 'by cause of death', or by means of any codicil or any pieces of writing whatsoever. They would also make those who held office in their palaces subject to a very harsh punishment in accordance with their rank, so that, stripped of every privilege pertaining to their position, they would incur disgrace, and persons of this kind would realize that they were subject to the same law as everyone else. Also, a penalty of thirty pounds of silver was enacted for the officials of the various judges, and if it came to pass that they persisted in their error and paid the penalty on five occasions, then were such people, having been convicted and beaten into submission by rods, to be eventually sent into exile.

10 "They went on to order that all the books of the priests whom they persecuted were to be cast into the fires, and we order that this is to be done in the case of books of this kind, from which their bad people argue for their erroneous belief. It is said that they ordered that these things were to be observed with respect to each individual person: the *illustres* were each to pay fifty pounds of gold, *spectabiles* forty pounds of gold, senators thirty pounds of gold, leading men twenty pounds of gold, priests thirty pounds of gold, decurions five pounds of gold, merchants five pounds of gold, common people five pounds of gold, and *circumcelliones*[6] ten pounds of silver; and if any persons happened to persist in this wickedness, all their goods were to be confiscated and they were to be punished with exile.

11 "We see that they afflicted the governing classes of the cities, as well as the overseers and the leaseholders[7] of the estates, with a penalty of this kind: if it happened that they were pleased to hide such people and had not made them public, and did not have them held fast

---

[6]   It is not clear whether these people are to be seen as an essentially religious phenomenon (so Calderone 1967) or as agricultural labourers (so Courtois 1955:147); see recently Frend 1982:618-20. The list of payments is broadly similar to one imposed on the Donatists in *cod theod* 16.5.52. The survival of the categories of people listed here is discussed by Clover (1982, esp. 667).

[7]   For the *conductores*, Decret/Fantar 1981:228f.

and presented for judgment, they themselves were to discharge the penalty. This was the punishment enacted for the leaseholders on the royal estates: by way of punishment they would be forced to render to the fisc as much as they paid to the royal household. This, we determine, is to be observed in general in the cases of all leaseholders and proprietors of land who believe they should persist in the same superstition. With respect to judges who failed to devote themselves to this matter with due urgency, proscription and capital punishment would be imposed as their penalty; the three chief officials of their departments were also to be punished, and the others condemned to a fine of twenty pounds of gold.

12 "Wherefore it is necessary for all homousians, who are known to have held and continue to hold to the substance of an evil persuasion of this kind, to be bound by these regulations: we decree that they are to abstain from all the things mentioned above, which, among the governing classes of all our towns, will entail prosecution; this is also to apply to judges who are found to be negligent in inflicting dire penalties on individual people. Therefore we order all those involved in the errors of the abovementioned homousian faith, which has been condemned by all of the many bishops in a council, to desist from every one of the aforementioned practices and legal agreements. They should know that nothing is allowed them; but a similar punishment is to remain in force and bind them all, if they are not converted to that true religion which we venerate and practise by 1 June in the eighth year of our reign. Our goodness has appointed this specific day so that indulgence may not be denied those who renounce their error, and fitting penalties may correct obstinate minds.

13 "But those who remain in the same error who either perform duties in our household or happen to be in charge of various administrative tasks are to be forced to submit to the monetary penalties described above in accordance with their grades, and things which they may have obtained through any kind of trickery will be of no use at all. With regard to private persons of whatever standing and position, this our decree orders that what is clearly stated in the abovementioned laws concerning such people is to be observed, so that they may be subjected to a fitting punishment. And we enjoin that judges of the

provinces who are negligent in carrying out what has been decreed are
to be liable to the punishment prescribed above for such people.

14 "And by this decree we ordain that all the churches of the entire
clergy of the abovementioned persuasion situated throughout the lands
and regions which are possessed by the governance of our sovereignty,
in accordance with the divine will, together with the property which
pertains to the same, ought to be of service to the true worshippers of
the divine majesty, that is our priests, not doubting that what is justly
bestowed on our sacred pontiffs will be of more use for the support of
the poor. We therefore order that this law, flowing from the fount of
justice, is to be made known to all, so that no-one can allege that he
is ignorant of what has been prescribed. May all go well with you!
Given at Carthage on 25 February."

15 After these deadly edicts, full of toxic poison, he ordered that all
the bishops who had come together at Carthage and whose churches,
homes and property they had already taken, were to be despoiled in
the lodgings where they were. After they had been despoiled, they were
to be driven outside the walls. Not an animal, not a slave, not so much
as the clothes on their backs was left them; furthermore, no-one was
to take any of them into his house or provide them with food. Anyone
who tried to do this out of pity was to be consumed by fire, together
with his entire household.

16 The bishops who had been cast forth then behaved wisely, for even
though they were now beggars they did not go away from where they
were. This was partly because, if they did go away, they could have
been forcibly called back and a false claim would be made, just as it
was made, that they had fled from the debate. But the chief reason was
that there was now nothing at all left where they would have returned,
their churches, property and homes having been taken over. Now, when
they were lying around the walls in the open air and groaning, it
happened that the wicked king went out on his way to the pool where
he used to swim. They all chose to run up to him, saying: "Why are we
oppressed in this way? What evil deeds have we done for us to be
enduring these things? If we were brought together in order to dispute,
why have we been despoiled, why have we been moved away, why have

we been dispersed, and why, separated from our churches and homes, are we suffering outside the city in hunger and nakedness,[8] wallowing in the midst of dung?" He looked on them with wild eyes, and before he had given a hearing to what they had to say he ordered that the horses, with their riders, were to be set upon them, with such violence that they could not only have been trampled upon, but also killed. Many of them, especially the old and infirm, were trampled upon at that time.

17 Then those men of God were ordered to proceed to a place called the temple of Memoria. They did not know of the trap which had been prepared for them. When they had come there they were shown a rolled-up document, and they were told, with subtlety worthy of the serpent: "Our lord king Hunirix, although he is distressed that in your contempt you are still holding back from obeying his will by becoming adherents of the religion which is his, has nevertheless had a good thought concerning you. If you will swear to carry out what is contained in this document, he bids you return to your churches and homes." To this, the bishops replied all together: "At all times we say, have said and shall say: We are Christians, we are bishops, we hold the one, true apostolic faith!"

18 After they had made this confession of faith there was a short silence, and then the men who had been chosen by the king made haste to obtain the oath from the bishops by force. Then those true men, the blessed bishops Hortulanus and Florentianus, spoke on behalf of them all and for them all: "Surely we are not unreasoning animals that will easily and thoughtlessly swear without knowing what the document contains?" The men chosen by the king immediately made known to them the contents of the piece of writing, decked out in words of this kind.

---

[8] A quote from Zeno (*CCSL* 22:149.144f). I owe this reference to Löfstedt 1982:72.

19 That piece of chicanery read as follows: "Swear that, after the death of our lord the king, you wish his son Hildirit[9] to be king, and that none of you will send letters to lands across the sea, for if you give your oath concerning this, he will restore you to your churches." In their good-hearted simplicity, many decided to give the oath, contrary to the divine prohibition, in case the people of God were later to say that the bishops who had not wished to swear were to blame for the churches not being restored. But other, more astute bishops felt that it was a deceptive trap, and were totally unwilling to swear. They said that it had been prohibited by the authority of the gospel, when the Lord himself says: 'Do not swear at all.' (Matt 5:13) The king's servants said to them: "Let those who are prepared to swear step aside." When they had done this shorthand writers took down what each one said and from which town he came; the same thing happened with those who did not swear. Each group was immediately delivered into custody.

20 But afterwards the trick which had been concealed became clear. To those who had sworn they said: "Because you were willing to swear, contrary to the precept of the gospel, the king has ordered that you are never to see your towns and churches, but are to be banished with the status of *coloni* and given fields to cultivate. As well, you are not to sing the psalms or pray or hold in your hands a book to read from; you are not to baptize or ordain, nor are you to dare to reconcile anyone." Similarly, it was said to those who had not sworn: "You did not want to swear because you do not wish the son of our lord to reign. For this reason an order has been given for you to be banished to the island of Corsica, so you can cut timber for the king's ships."

21 That beast, a thirst for the blood of the innocent,[10] went further. At a time when those bishops had not yet been sent into exile, he sent simultaneously through all the provinces of the land of Africa most cruel torturers, so that there did not remain a single home or place free of wailing and lamentations. They did not spare people of any age or

---

[9] So spelt by Victor; the form Hilderic is more usual. The possibility that the bishops had been involved in plots is discussed by Courtois 1955:294f.

[10] Courcelle 1964: 188 n.5 sees here a reference to the Beast of Revelation.

either sex, except those who submitted to their will. Some were tortured by being beaten, others by being hung, and others by the fire; contrary to the laws of nature, women, especially the noble, were tortured entirely naked and in full view of the public.

22 Of these I shall mention one, our Dionysia, in a quick and concise manner. When they saw that she was not only more courageous but also more beautiful than the other married women, they set to work first on her, to strip her and get her ready for the clubs. Trusting in her Lord she put up with these things and said: "Torture me however you like, but do not uncover those parts which would cause me shame." They, behaving still more wildly, stripped off all her clothes and made her stand up in a more prominent place, making a spectacle of her in front of everyone. Amid the blows of the rods, and while streams of blood were already flowing over her whole body, she spoke in a bold voice: "You servants of the Devil, what you think you are doing to my shame is in fact to my praise." And because she had a full knowledge of the divine scriptures, she strengthened others for their martyrdom, despite having been afflicted with punishments and being already a martyr herself. By her holy example she set nearly the whole of her country free.

23 When she saw that her only son, who was still of tender years and rather delicate, was afraid and in dread of the punishments, she strengthened him by casting wounding glances and threatening him with her motherly authority[11] to such an extent that he was turned into someone far stronger than his mother. When he was in the midst of the cruel scourges she spoke to him in this way: "Remember, my son, that we have been baptized in the catholic mother in the name of the Trinity. Let us not lose that garment of our salvation, in case the host, when he comes, does not find the wedding garment and says to his servants: 'Cast him into the outer darkness, where there will be weeping and gnashing of teeth.' (Matt 22:13) The punishment to be feared is the one which will never end, and the life to be desired is the

---

[11] I read 'auctoritate materna', with Petschenig, against 'aeterna'. Such expressions are formulaic with Victor: cf. 'materno...affectu' (2.29) and 'auctoritate uxoria' (3.50).

one which will be enjoyed for ever." So it was that, strengthening her son by words such as these, she quickly made a martyr of him.

24   That young man, so worthy of veneration, whose name was Majoricus, breathed his last in the struggle he waged for his confession and completed his palm-strewn course. The woman, embracing the victim, truly hers, rendered thanks to the Lord with as many words as she was capable of, and she chose to bury him, in the joy of future hope, in her home, so that as often as she poured forth her prayers to the Trinity above his tomb, she would be confident that she was never far from her son. It would take long to tell how many were the people who, as we have said, were gained for God through her in that town. For there were also her sister, named Dativa, and Leontia, the daughter of the holy bishop Germanus, and Emilius, one of Dativa's relations, a doctor worthy of reverence, as well as the religious man Tertius, who was outstanding for his confession of the Trinity, and Boniface of Sibida. So many were the things they suffered, and such were the torments with which they were tortured, that one who is capable should speak of them one at a time.

25   And who could tell the story of the punishments which Servus, from the large town of Tuburbo (Henchir Kasbat), a true man, eminent and noble, endured for Christ? After receiving countless blows from rods he was frequently lifted up by machines with pulleys and, as he hung, taken throughout the city for the whole day. Now he was lifted on high, but when the ropes were released again he fell quickly and tumbled down with the full weight of his body on the pebbles of the streets, coming down upon the stones like a stone. But more often he was dragged along and made to rub against stones which were very sharp, so that his skin came off and you would see it hanging from his body along his sides, back and belly. He had already suffered things quite like these in the time of Geiseric, for not making public the secrets of a particular friend: how much more would he suffer now, when he was safeguarding the mysteries of his faith? And if he faithfully displayed his faith for the sake of a man, and for no gain, how much more must he have done so for the sake of the one who will render to him a reward for that faith?

26 But I lack the ability to narrate the deeds which were accomplished
in the town of Culusi, because it is beyond human power even to count
the number of martyrs and confessors there. In that place there was a
married woman, Victoria, who conformed to her name. While she was
being tortured by being left hanging for a good while in the sight of the
common people, she was addressed in the following terms by her
husband, already a lost man, in the presence of their children: "Why
are you suffering, wife? If you hold me in disdain, at least have mercy
on these little ones to whom you gave birth, you evil woman! Why do
you forget your womb and count as nothing those you bore amidst
groans? Where are the covenants of married love? Where are the
bonds of that relationship which written documents once brought about
between us, in accordance with the law which pertains to respectable
folk? Look, I beseech you, on your children and husband, and hasten
to comply with what is commanded in the king's order, so that you may
escape the torments still to come and, as well, be given back to me and
our children." But she, listening to neither the wailing of her children
nor the blandishments of the serpent, lifted her affections far above the
earth and despised the world with its desires. When those who had
been torturing her saw that she had died, her shoulders having been
wrenched away owing to the period for which she had hung,
straightaway they took her down, completely lifeless. Afterwards she
said that a virgin had stood by her and touched her limbs, one by one,
and she had been healed then and there.

27 I do not know how to commend Victorianus, a citizen of the town
of Hadrumentum (Sousse) who was then proconsul of Carthage; words
fail me. There was no-one more wealthy than he in the regions of
Africa, and even the wicked king considered him a most faithful man
in the things which were always being entrusted to him. In a friendly
way the king sent word to him and he was told that he would be
considered the first among all if he would readily give assent to what
he enjoined. But with great confidence that man of God replied to the
people sent to him thus: "Trusting as I do in Christ, my God and my

Lord,[12] I tell you what you are to tell the king: let him make me stand
in the fires, let him drive me to the beasts, let him afflict me with
torments of every kind; if I consent, I have been baptized in the
catholic church in vain. For even if this present life were the only one
and we did not hope for the other life, eternal and true, I would not
act in such a way as to enjoy glory for a short and passing period while
being ungrateful to my creditor who had faith in me." The tyrant was
aroused at his answer and afflicted him with punishments which lasted
so long and were so great that human speech could not set them forth.
Rejoicing in the Lord he came to a good end, and so received a
martyr's crown.

28 But who would have the ability to set forth the contests which the
martyrs also waged in the town of Thambaia? There it was that two
brothers who came from the town of Aqua Regia, trusting in the Lord,
took an oath together that they would ask the torturers to inflict upon
them the one punishment and an equal suffering. And when, having
been hung up for the first time, they had been suspended all day with
heavy stones tied to their feet, one of them asked to be let down and
given some respite. The other brother feared that he would renounce
the faith, and called out to him from where he hung: "Don't, don't,
brother! This is not what we have sworn to Christ. I shall accuse you
when we come before his dreadful throne, because we swore upon his
Body and Blood that we would suffer for him together." Saying these
and many other things he strengthened his brother for the combat of
his passion, and the latter, crying out in a loud voice, proclaimed:
"Unleash whatever sufferings you like, and torment the Christians with
cruel punishments: what my brother will do, I shall do as well." With
how many red-hot plates they burned them, with what kinds of claws[13]
they dug into them, and with what torments they tortured them is made

---

[12] Reading 'de Christo deo et domino meo' with Halm, against 'de deo et Christo domino
meo' (Petschenig). The latter reading may represent an attempt to make better theological
sense, but the high Christology implied by the former is suggested elsewhere by Victor (3.63),
with which compare Joh 20:28 and II Thess 1:12, and, in Hydatius, the expression 'servus Iesu
Christi dei et domini nostri' (*MGH AA* 11:13.5). It is clearly anti-Arian in tendency.

[13] The *ungula* was a form of torture traditionally used against Christians: Tertullian *apol*
12.4, 30.7; Cyprian *ep* 21.4; Prudentius *peristef* 1.44.

clear by this fact: the torturers themselves 'cast them out of their sight' (cf Ps 50:13 Vulg), saying: "The entire people imitates them, so that no-one at all is converted to our religion." This was especially so, because no bruises and no traces whatever of their punishments were to be seen on them.

29 But let us go on quickly to tell what was done to the glory of God in the town of Tipasa (Tifech) in greater Mauritania. When they saw that a former notary of Cyrila had been ordained as the Arian bishop for their town, to the perdition of souls, the entire town fled together all at once on the next sailing to Spain, leaving behind only a few who had not been able to sail.[14] The bishop of the Arians began to put pressure on these people, first by blandishments and later by threats, in an attempt to make Arians of them. But they were strong in the Lord: not only did they laugh at the madness of the man who was exhorting them, but they also began to celebrate the divine mysteries in public, gathering together in a house. When the bishop found out about this, in secret he sent to Carthage a report about it which was hostile to them.

30 When this came to the attention of the king, in his wrath he sent a count with orders that the entire province was to be gathered together in the middle of the forum, and that he was to cut the tongues and right hands of these people completely off. But when this was done, thanks to the operation of the Holy Spirit they spoke, and continue to speak, just as they had spoken before. And if anyone finds this hard to believe, he should go to Constantinople now, and there he will find one of them, the subdeacon Reparatus, speaking correctly and in a faultless manner. For this reason he is held to be worthy of reverence in the palace of the emperor Zeno, and the queen in particular venerates him with an extraordinary devotion.[15]

---

[14] On the links between Tipasa and Spain, Courtois 1954:30. The town was a long way from the chief area of Vandal settlement.

[15] In various forms this story circulated widely; see Procopius *BV* 1.8.4, followed by Evagrius *hist eccl* 4.14; Victor of Tunnunna *chron s.a.* 479.1; Marcellinus comes *chron s.a.* 484; *cod just* 1.27.1.4; Aeneas of Gaza (*PG* 85:1001A); Gregory the Great *dial* 3.32, (where the incident is curiously dated to the time of Justinian). Marrou, with reference to the evidence of

31 But who could describe in fitting language or confine himself to just a brief account of the different punishments which the Vandals, on the order of the king, inflicted on their own people? If a writer tried to recount the things which were done in Carthage itself one by one, without any ornament of speech, he would not even be able to indicate the names of the torments. The evidence can easily be viewed today. You can look upon people without hands, others without eyes, others who have no feet, others whose noses and ears have been cut off; and you can see others, left hanging for too long a period, whose heads, which used to be held normally, have been plunged between their shoulders, and who have protruding shoulder blades. This occurred because they tortured some by hanging them from high buildings and swinging them to and fro through the empty air by jerking ropes with their hands. In some cases the ropes broke, and those who had been hung so high fell down with great force. Many of these people lost their skulls, together with their eyes; others died immediately, their bones broken; while others expired shortly afterwards.

32 But if anyone thinks this is just a story, he should ask Uranius, the legate of Zeno, in whose presence these things were chiefly done. The reason, it is clear, was as follows: when he came to Carthage, he boasted that he had come to defend the catholic churches. And the tyrant, to show him that he was afraid of no-one, stationed torturers, greater in number and more cruel, in those streets and quarters which legates generally pass through as they go up to the palace and come down.[16] This conduct was clearly to the opprobrium of the empire and of our age, now nearing its end.[17]

33 So it was that the wife of one of the king's butlers, Dagila by name, who had already been a prominent confessor on many occasions during the times of Geiseric, a noble and elegant woman, was thoroughly

---

the Russian Old Believers of the seventeenth century, comments that it is not unknown for people to speak after their tongues have been pulled out (1967:207).

[16] On the route legates would have taken, Clover 1982a:8, with Procopius *BV* 1.20.21 and 2.2.7.9 on people going up to the palace.

[17] Victor uses 'res publica' for the empire. On the use of 'faex' in this passage, *TLL* 6:171.49f.

disabled by whips and cudgels and then banished to an arid and impenetrable place of exile, where no-one would be able to come and bring her comfort. With joy she left her home, and her husband and children as well. It is said that she was later given the opportunity of being moved to a less harsh part of the desert where, if she wished, she would enjoy the support of companions. But she, believing that great joy was already hers there, where no human sympathy could bring her comfort, asked that this not be done.

34 Then, when the shepherd Eugenius had already been exiled as well,[18] the entire clergy of the church of Carthage, some 500 or more, weakened by flogging and lack of food, were also driven, as they rejoiced in the Lord, far away in a cruel exile. Among them were many lectors, mere children.[19] But I must not remain silent concerning the freedom displayed by the deacon Muritta, who acted more freely than the others, while they were being flogged in the middle of the city. There was also a man called Elpidoforus, very cruel and ferocious, who had been given the job of tearing in pieces the limbs of the confessors of Christ, as he tortured them with violence. Some time previously, and while I was present, he had been baptized in the church of Faustus, and the venerable deacon Muritta had taken him up, regenerate, from the depths of the font. But afterwards, when he had forsaken his religion, he showed such great savageness towards the church of God that he was found to be worse than all the others in the way he carried out the persecution.

35 Why go into details? First of all the priests were summoned, in order, to be tormented by tortures, and, after the archdeacon Salutaris, punishments were imposed on the Muritta we have mentioned, for he was second in rank among the junior clergy.[20] As Elpidoforus sat by

---

[18] That Eugenius was exiled to Tamalleni may be deduced from the *Notitia provinciarum civitatum Africae, procons* 1; see further below 3.43f. An apparently authentic letter from him to the people of Carthage is reproduced by Gregory of Tours *hist franc* 2.3.

[19] For lectors as children, see *brevarium hipponense* can 18 (*CCSL* 259:38, with 298 no. 129). Epiphanius, later bishop of Pavia, became a lector when eight: Ennodius *V Epi* 8.

[20] 'Ministri', a word already used at 1.37 and 1.51. From the context here it clearly means those clergy holding a rank lower than that of priest.

muttering, they began to stretch out the old man, worthy of honour. His clothes had not yet been taken off, and in secret, with no-one knowing, he was carrying the linen towels in which he had wrapped Elpidoforus when he had taken him up from the font. He brandished these and held them up in view of everyone, and when he spoke the following words he is said to have moved the entire town to lamentation and tears.

36 "These are the linen cloths, Elpidoforus, you servant of falsehood, which will accuse you when the Judge comes in his majesty. I shall be careful to keep them as a testimony of your perdition, so that you will be sunk in the abyss of the sulphurous pit. They clad you when you rose spotless from the font, and they will follow after you the more bitterly when you begin to possess a flaming gehenna, because you have 'put on a curse just like a garment' (Ps 108:18), breaking asunder and letting go of the sacrament of true baptism and faith. What are you going to do, you miserable man, when the servants of the head of the family begin to bring together the people invited to the king's supper? Then the king, with frightening indignation, will see that you, a person who was at one time invited, have taken off the wedding garment, and he will say to you: 'Friend, how have you come hither without a wedding garment?' (Matt 22:12) I do not see that which I conferred on you; I do not recognize what I gave. You have lost the cloak worn by my soldiery, which I wove on the loom of virgin limbs for ten months, stretched out on the fuller's stretcher of the cross, cleansed with water, and beautified with the purple dye of my blood. I do not discern the adornment of my sign; I do not see the branding mark[21] of the Trinity. Such a man will not be able to take part in my banquet.

37 "'Bind him hand and foot with his cords, because of his own free will he has desired to separate himself from the Catholics who were formerly his brothers. He 'spread out ropes' tied together 'to be a

---

[21] For 'character' as the branding mark imposed on Christians in baptism, see *TLL* 3:992.77ff; the usage is particularly common in Augustine. The 'wedding garment' is therefore the sacrament of baptism, which Elpidoforus has presumably lost by being rebaptized; cf above 2.23. The issue of rebaptism is constant for much of book three. The 'sign' ('signaculum') referred to immediately above is the sign of the cross.

snare' (cf Ps 139:6), but with them he has both bound himself and prevented others from coming to that feast. 'He placed a stumbling block' for many 'alongside the path' (cf Ps 139:6), and now I have cast him forth from my feast, in perpetual disgrace and to his eternal shame.'" While Muritta said these and other things, Elpidoforus was speechless, roasted by the fire of his conscience before he experienced the fire which is eternal.

38 So it was that all of them, making their backs ready for the rods, quickly went forth into exile. While they were still making their long journey, at the prompting of the bishops of the Arians, men were sent, pitiless and violent, so that any food which the kindness of Christians happened to bring them would be cruelly taken away. Then each one of them quite boldly sang: "'Naked I came forth from my mother's womb' (Job 1:21), and it is fitting that I also go forth into exile naked, because the Lord knows how to provide food for the hungry and to clothe those in the wilderness." Furthermore two Vandals, oftentimes confessors under Geiseric, despised all their wealth and proceeded into exile with these clerics, in the company of their mother.

39 But at the prompting of that lost man Teucharius, who had formerly been a lector, twelve little children were, in accordance with what he said, separated from that multitude of confessors who were on the move, that is, the clergy of the church of Carthage. He knew that they were powerful singers and skilled at singing rhythmically, for they had been his pupils when he had been a Catholic. As soon as he had made the suggestion they were sent away on fast post horses, and the dozen children were called back from their journey by the power of barbarian raging. They were separated from the flock of the saints in body but not in spirit; fearing that they would fall, they took hold of the knees of their companions with sighs and tears, so that they would not be torn away. Nevertheless, the violent heretics separated them by threatening them with swords and summoned them back to Carthage.

40 But they were not treated with the kindly acts appropriate to those of such an age, and they were found older than their years. 'So that they would not fall asleep in death' (cf Ps 12:4) they lit the lamp of evangelical light. The Arians, filled with indignation, blushed at having

been overcome by children. Aroused by this, they ordered that those on whom they had inflicted various floggings just a few days previously were again to be subjected to the rods. Wounds were imprinted on wounds, and the torment, as it was renewed, grew worse. It turned out that, with the Lord providing strength, despite their youth they did not give way to the pain, but rather their morale, strengthened in the faith, grew. Carthage now cherishes them with a wondrous love, and looks on the band of children as the twelve apostles. They live as one, they eat at the same time, they sing the psalms as a group, and they glorify the Lord at the same time.

41 In those days two merchants from the same town, Frumentius and another Frumentius, were crowned with an outstanding martyrdom. It was then too that seven men, brothers not by nature but by grace, who dwelt together in a monastery, finished their struggle as confessors and came to an unfading crown. They were abbot Liberatus, the deacon Boniface, the subdeacons Servus and Rusticus, and the monks Rogatus, Septimus and Maximus.[22]

42 Now at that time the bishops, priests and clergy of the Arians were raging with greater cruelty than the king and the Vandals.[23] For they themselves, with their clergy, were running everywhere, girded with swords, in order to persecute. Among them was a bishop, more cruel than the others, named Antonius; so abominable and unbelievable are the things which he did to us that they cannot be told. He lived in a town near the desert, not far from the province of Tripolitania, and, like a beast which could not be satisfied and thirsted for the blood of Catholics, he ran to and fro, roaring, in order to snatch them. (cf I Pet 5:18)

43 The wicked Huniric, knowing how fierce Antonius was, decided to banish the holy Eugenius to those parts of the desert. When Antonius had taken him into custody he kept watch over him so closely that no-

---

[22] These are the seven men whose *passio* is related in a work which may have been by Victor. See further, on a commemorative inscription, Bairam-Ben and Ennabli 1982.

[23] One of a number of indications in these chapters that not all Arians were Vandals. Evidence for Roman converts to Arianism is discussed by Koenig 1981:335, 341-44.

one was permitted to go in to him. He also considered how he might kill him by tormenting him with different plots and punishments. But the holy Eugenius wept at the misfortunes of those of us who were undergoing persecution, and wore down his old body with a rough garment of hair. Lying on the bare ground, 'he wet his couch with showers of tears' (Ps 6:7), and at length he experienced a dangerous attack of paralysis.

44 On being told of this the Arian became joyful, and quickly he made his way to the place, somewhat apart, where the man of God was in exile. When he saw the true pontiff, burdened with his suffering, produce a few stammering words, he decided then and there to deprive of his life a man whom he did not wish to go on living. He ordered that vinegar, bitter and exceedingly strong, was to be obtained, and when it had been brought he poured it into the throat, reluctant and unwilling, of the venerable old man. For if the Lord of all, who came for the very purpose of drinking, did not wish to drink something which he had tasted, how much more would that servant and faithful confessor have been totally unwilling?[24] But heretical savageness poured it in. The vinegar was particularly harmful to him in the condition he was in, and his disease became worse. But in his goodness Christ mercifully came to his aid and later restored his health.

45 Events made clear how much trouble he could cause another of our bishops, the similarly banished Habetdeum of the town of Thamalluma, where Antonius was. Having afflicted him with different kinds of persecutions and been unable to make an Arian of him, and seeing the soldier of Christ ever constant in his confession, he made a promise to his people, saying "Unless I make him an adherent of our religion, I am not Antonius." When he was found wanting in his promise, he planned something else which the Devil put into his mind.

46 He harassed the bishop, whose feet and hands he had bound in huge chains, and having stopped up his mouth in case he cried out he sprinkled water, which he thought was the water of rebaptism, on his

---

[24] A reminiscence of the narratives of Christ's passion; see Matt 27:34,48.

body. As if he could bind the conscience as he bound the body, or as if the one 'who hears the groans of the shackled' (Ps 101:21) and scrutinizes the secrets of the heart was not close by, or as if deceptive water could overcome the resolve of the firm intention which the man of God had already sent to heaven as an ambassador, accompanied by tears! Immediately he released the man from his chains and, rejoicing, proceeded to speak in these terms: "Lo, brother Habetdeum, you have now been made one of our Christians. What else could you have done, if you were in agreement with the will of the king?" Habetdeum replied to him: "Evil Antonius, the damnation of death occurs where the assent of the will is bound. I, resolute in my faith, have frequently confessed in words and defended with shouts what I believe and have believed. But after you bound me in chains and stopped up the entrance to my mouth, even then in the palace of my heart I prepared a report concerning the violence I have suffered. The angels wrote it down, and I sent it to my Emperor for him to read."

47 Indeed, the violence of the tyrants was universal, for Vandals had been sent everywhere for the purpose of handing over people travelling along the roads to their priests so that they would be slaughtered. But, when they had slain them with the sword of deceiving water, they gave them a document written in testimony of their perdition, in case they were dragged away with similar violence on another occasion, because neither private citizens nor merchants were allowed to travel anywhere unless the wretched people displayed a written token of their death. In former times Christ already showed this through a revelation to his servant John, when he says: 'No-one will be allowed to buy or sell anything unless he has the branding mark of the beast on his forehead and on his hand.'(cf Rev 13:16f)

48 For their bishops and priests went round the villages and towns by night with an armed band, and when these robbers of souls had forced open the doors they made their way in, bearing water and the sword. Those whom they found at home, some of them lying asleep in bed, they besprinkled with a fiery and destructive shower, shouting as if they were demons and calling them Christians of the same kind as themselves, so demonstrating that their heresy is a game rather than any religion. The less intelligent and the ignorant thought that because

of this they were guilty of defilement from sacrilege, but the wiser rejoiced that it had not harmed them, because it had been done against their will and while they were asleep. Many straightaway scattered ashes on their heads, and others, in their sorrow at what had happened, clad themselves in hair shirts. Some plastered themselves with filthy mud and tore into shreds the linen cloths[25] which had been put on them by force, and with the hand of faith they threw them into cesspits and foul places.

49 I was looking on when a noble man's son, about seven years old, was separated from his parents here at Carthage with violence of the same kind, on the orders of Cyrila. His mother, laying aside womanly modesty, let down her hair and ran after the abductors through the whole city, while the little child cried out as best he could: "I am a Christian! I am a Christian! By means of S Stephen, I am a Christian!"[26] But they closed his mouth and plunged him, guiltless child that he was, into their whirlpool.

50 The same thing is known to have happened to the children of a well-regarded doctor, Liberatus. For when the king commanded that he be sent into exile with his wife and children, in their wickedness the Arians decided to separate the little children from their parents, seeking to use the influence of love to overthrow the strength of the parents. The young children, those tender pledges of their marriage, were separated from their parents. When Liberatus wanted to cry, he was rebuked by the authority of his wife, and his tears immediately dried up in their very ducts. For his wife said to him: "And are you going to lose your soul because of the children, Liberatus? Consider them as not having been born, for Christ will claim them entirely for himself. Don't you see them shouting and saying 'We are Christians!'?"

51 What this woman did in the sight of the judges should not be passed over in silence. For when she and her husband were being held

---

[25] 'Linteamina'; the reference is to the garments in which the newly baptized were clad. The same word is used at 3.36.

[26] On the cult of S Stephen, Duval 1982:624-32.

in prison separately so that they did not see each other at all, a message was sent to the wife and she was told: "Relax your harshness, for behold, your husband has obeyed the command of the king and become one of our Christians." But she said: "Let me see him and I, too, shall do as God wills." She was therefore taken from the prison and found her husband bound and standing with a great throng before the tribunals. Thinking that what the enemies had made up was true, she threw out her hand, grabbed the edges of his clothes next to his throat and, as everyone looked on, proceeded to choke him, saying: "You abandoned reprobate, unworthy of the grace of God and of his mercy, why have you wished to enjoy glory for a little while and perish for eternity? How will gold, how will silver be of any use to you? Is it really possible that they will free you from the furnace of hell?" She said many other things as well. But her husband replied to her: "Why are you suffering, wife? What does it look like? Whatever have you been hearing about me? I remain a catholic in the name of Christ, and I shall never be able to let go of what I hold." The heretics, aware that their falsehood had been uncovered, were then totally unable to gloss over their deceit.

52 We have spoken briefly above of their violent cruelty. Many people, both men and women, were afraid of this and hid themselves away, some in caves and others in uninhabited places, where no-one knew about them. There, lacking the food needed to sustain them, they were overcome by hunger and cold, and expired in their crushed and oppressed state. But amid these unwelcome afflictions they remained firm, their faith inviolate. So it was that Cresconius, a priest of the town of Mizeita (Ain Babouch), was found in a cave of Mount Ziquense, already freed from his rotting body.

53 We have spoken already about the holy Habetdeum. Afterwards he made his way to Carthage, thinking that he would approach the evil king so that he might make manifest his conscience, which was always on close and friendly terms with the Trinity, before men as well. He was not a diffident man, and Antonius was not able to restrain him. He presented to the most wicked king a little book which contained words like these: "Tell me, what are you doing with those already banished? Why do you struggle each day with those whom you send into exile?

You have taken away their property and deprived them of their churches, fatherland and homes. Only the soul remains, and you are doing your best to take this captive. O the times, O the manners![27] The whole world understands these things, and he who takes vengeance sees them. If what you hold is called faith, why do you disturb the members of the true faith with such great persecutions? What are you doing concerning our exile, what are you doing with us, the needy of this world, whose life is always in Christ? Those whom you have cast away from the sight of all people should at least be allowed to enjoy the company of the beasts!"

54   When the pontiff of God had said these and similar things, the accursed tyrant is said to have given him this order: "Go to our bishops and carry out what they tell you, because they are known to have total power in this matter." Not even this circumstance, however, could call Antonius back from his insanity, because he knew that through his conduct he could please the wicked king a great deal. But bishop Habetdeum, rejoicing in having satisfied his conscience, preferred to return to his place of exile.

55   At that time a famine occurred which was beyond belief, and it began to devastate the whole of Africa, laying it all waste. There was no rain then; not a single drop fell from heaven. This did not happen for no reason, but in accordance with the true and just judgment of God, so that where, because of the persecuting Arians, the water of the muddy whirlpool[28] had bubbled with fire and sulphur, the rain which heaven bestows in its kindness and which had always been abundantly to hand was withheld. The whole face of the earth remained yellowish: the vine was not covered with leaves during a shaded summer; the measures of grain which were scattered did not make the countenance of the fields green; the olive tree, which is always green and full of pleasant leaves, did not have its usual elegant covering; the thickets of

---

[27] 'O tempora, O mores!' is a quotation from Cicero *cat* 1.2, but neither this nor the two reminiscences of Vergil in following chapters (3.62f) prove that Victor, or indeed bishop Habetdeum, had first hand knowledge of these classical authors.

[28] Juvenal 3.266, probably known to Victor from Zeno 1.4.2; see *TLL* 3:97.5ff, with Löfstedt 1982:72.

fruit trees did not bring forth gems of flowers on the fructifying earth and go on to yield fruit, as they usually do.

56 Everything was dismal and repulsive, and the disaster, which was on the scale of a pestilence, brought about the ruin of all Africa. The earth totally failed to produce the green of germinating plants for either humankind or beasts. (cf Ps 103:14) The beds of rivers which, not long before, had been running with a strong flow, became dry; the rippling watercourses of the fountains, deprived of their perennial sources, became equally dry. 'All the sheep and oxen, as well as the beasts of the field' (Ps 8:8), and likewise the forest animals, were never seen at all, as hunger put an end to them. And where there happened to be a grassy field, located in a valley which was still moist, which began to display the colour of new hay, pallid rather than green, in that place a burning and fiery wind sprang up, drying out everything with its scorching, because the dusty weather, which caused everything under the dry air to shrivel up, had cast a cloud over every place.

57 There was no buying and selling at that time, and the sods of the earth were not turned as the bullocks pulled the plough, because there were no cattle available and absolutely no villages remained. But when one group of country people died, those who happened to have survived were already waiting for burial. And because, as we have said, owing to the wretched constraint of hunger, the usual trade did not take place, and the due cultivation was not bestowed on the fields, marching bands and funeral processions of young and old, of youths and maidens, of boys and even girls were spread about everywhere, going around towns, villages and individual cities, to whatever place and by whatever means they found possible. 'For they were turned in a perverse direction and, provoking God at the water of contradiction, they endured hunger like dogs' (cf Ps 77:57, 105:32, 58:7), not that they might eat bread, but so that they might feel the bitter hostility of the Trinity whom they denied.

58 Some were scattered across the plains, others sought secret places in the woods, looking for old grass roots and other waste things. There were large numbers who, when they tried to leave their homes, collapsed on the threshold, overcome by hunger, so that the streets and

lanes were filled with corpses, and as they moved about the living were
killed on every side by the stench of the dead. Every day people
breathing their last died everywhere, but the survivors lacked the
strength to provide the burials mercy would have required. For those
who were alive were too few to bury them, and as hunger gained the
upper hand they themselves were to die shortly afterwards. Individuals
desired to change their own free status and that of their children to a
condition of perpetual servitude, but they were not able to find a way
of doing so. Mountains and hills, the streets of the towns, roads and
lanes constituted one and the same place of burial for all those people
whose lives were being taken away by the hunger which consumed
them.[29]

59   But the Vandals themselves, who had become wealthy from the
holding of Africa in the first place and, later, from the plentiful spoils
taken from many provinces, were tormented by a still greater want.
And the more magnificent they had seemed to themselves as they
accumulated slaves, the more were they weakened as hunger tormented
them. No-one held on to a child, a wife, or his own slave, but each one
went forth, not where he would but where he could, and either
immediately faltered or never came back at all.

60   A wretched crowd was driven to come together at the city of
Carthage itself. And when those still living corpses came together there
in large numbers and the king saw the heaps of the dead which could
not be carried away, he immediately ordered that they were all to be
driven from the city, in case infection from the dying caused his people
to have to be buried with them. He commanded that each was to be
sent back to his own province and home. But these were not people
capable of going back, since each one bore his own burial on his face.
And as it turned out, there was a greater loss among the rebaptized,
for this reason: while the Arians promised the completion of this
present life, this is not what happened, and a first death, which was

---

[29]   Dutch archaeologists have discovered remains suggestive of death by epidemic or
famine in late fifth century Africa: Clover 1982a:15f.

nevertheless a subsequent one, came before a second.[30] To such an extent did the devastating famine claim lordship for itself that some well inhabited places lost their populations; these places now repose in a deep silence, with only their walls standing.

61   But why do I linger over a topic I lack the ability to give an account of? For if they were still alive and it were proper for them to speak of such things, the river of Cicero's eloquence would be dried up, and Sallust would remain wholly speechless. And, to pass over strangers unworthy of so great a subject, if Eusebius of Caesarea, a man suitable for this task, were to rise up, or Rufinus, the translator of his Greek eloquence, a man adorned with Latin flowers...but why go on? Not Ambrose, not Jerome, not our Augustine himself would suffice. 'Hear these things, all peoples; give ear, all you who live on the earth, you born of the earth and sons of men, rich and poor all together.'(cf Ps 48:2f)

62   Those of you who love barbarians and sometimes praise them, in a way worthy of condemnation, give thought to their name and understand their ways.[31] Surely there is no name by which they could be appropriately called other than 'barbarian', a fitting word connoting savageness, cruelty and terror? However many may be the gifts with which you befriend them, and however many the acts of compliance with which you placate them, they can think of nothing other than looking on Romans with envy, and, to the extent that things turn out in accordance with their will, it is their constant desire to darken the brightness and nobility of the Roman name. They desire not a single one of the Romans to live. And in cases where it is known that they have spared their subjects until now, they spare them for to use as slaves: for they have never loved a single Roman.[32]

---

[30]   There is an allusion here to Rev 2:11, 20:6. The second death is also referred to above at 1.50.

[31]   Victor here attacks the point of view represented by Salvian in his *de gubernatione dei*, although it is not clear whether he knew this author's work; see Pastorino 1980:95-100.

[32]   Victor's attitude to Romans and barbarians has been discussed by Alfonsi:1976. The phrase 'spared their subjects' stems from Vergil *aen* 6.853, where it is applied to Romans. This allusion, together with the string of authors named in 3.61 and the reference to Mezentius in

63 If barbarian ferocity was concerned to dispute with us concerning
the faith, and if the Arian heresy would dispute in a reasonable way -
but when did it possess reason, separating as it does God the Son, the
Saviour, from God the Father? - why have they relied on plots and
false accusations and tried to turn everything upside down? The storm
of their rage has been like the wind of a tempest. If it was necessary
for the bishops to dispute, why the hangings, why the fires, why the
claws and the crosses? Why has the serpent-like progeny of the Arians
devised for use against the innocent such tortures as Mezentius himself
did not dream up?[33] A passionate desire for rage and a greed for
cruelty, which sought the loss of souls and the plunder of property,
contended against innocence. If it was a conference that was sought,
why the seizure of the property of others, not just of bishops but of all
the laity as well? But those people rejoiced at being despoiled and
received the seizure of their property with joy.

64 May there now be present, I ask, people of every age, sex and
condition of life; may there be present, I implore, the entire throng of
the catholic name carried in the womb of its mother (cf Is 46:3) across
the whole world, because it alone knows how to provide brotherly
sympathy, as is learned from Paul the teacher, 'rejoicing together with
those who are happy and lamenting with those who mourn.' (Rom
12:15) Let them come together at the house of our grief and let us
pour forth rivers of tears from our eyes together, because the matter
relates to the cause and faith we have in common.

65 I wish for no heretic to come and mourn with me, because he
might aspire 'to add to the pain of my wounds' (Ps 68:27) and daily
'take joy in my misfortunes' (Ps 34:26). I do not want, no, I do not
want the sympathy of strangers, but I seek that of brothers; I do not
want that of 'the sons of strangers whose mouth has spoken vanity and
their right hands are the right hands of iniquity' (Ps 143:7f), because
'the sons of strangers have' ever 'lied to me', those who 'became old

---

3.63, is a sign of the more literary style Victor adopts towards the end of his book.

[33] Mezentius was, according to Vergil, an ally of Aeneas' enemy Turnus. The tortures he
used are known from *aen* 8.481-87. Pastorino, on the strength of this reference asserts that
Victor knew Vergil (1980:79n.116), but I would rather keep an open mind.

and limped away from their paths.' (Ps 17:46 Vulg) They 'say to me daily "Where is your God?"' (Ps 41:4,11) while that people purchased by the precious Blood of the Lamb is struck down. Amid their reproaches I, 'prepared for the whips' (cf. Ps 37:11f Vulg), do not cease to sing to the Lord as he whips me, "Take your whips away from me, for 'I have been laid low', not 'by the strength of your hand' (Ps 38:12 Vulg), but by the persecution of the Arian heresy."

66 Let all who tread the path of the narrow way with me and who, 'on account of the words of the lips of God, keep to the hard paths', (cf Ps 16:14) come 'and see whether there is any grief like my grief.' (Lam 1:12) Since I am a gatherer of grapes for the day of the fierce anger of the Lord, 'all my enemies have opened their mouths against me, they have hissed and ground their teeth, and they have said: "We shall eat him up! This is the day we have been waiting for; we have come upon it, we have seen it!"' (Lam 2:16)

67 Be present, angels of my God, you who never fail, established as you are in your ministry for the sake of those who have taken hold of the inheritance of eternal salvation, and look upon all Africa, formerly supported by companies of great churches, now deprived of them all; then adorned with great ranks of priests, now sitting as a downcast widow. 'Its priests and elders have perished' in uninhabited places and islands 'from seeking food to eat' (Lam 1:19), but they did not find any. 'Pay attention and see' (cf. Lam 1:11) that Zion the city of our God 'has become contemptible and, as it were, polluted by menses in the midst of those hostile to her.' (cf Lam 1:17) 'The enemy has set his hand against all her desirable things, and so she sees the nations invading and entering into her courts, people who, you have ordered, are not to enter into your church.' (Lam 1:10) 'Her paths are in mourning, because no-one assembles on a festival day.' (Lam 1:4)

68 'All comeliness and charm has departed' (Lam 1:6 Vulg) from her face; 'her virgins' have learned to walk along bitter paths, 'and her young men,' brought up in the halls of monasteries; they 'have gone away into captivity' (Lam 1:18) among the Moors, while 'her holy stones are scattered,' not only 'at the corners of all the streets' (Lam 4:1), but also in the foul places of the mines. Say 'to God our

protector' (cf Ps 41:10), with the confidence of one at prayer, 'since she
is afflicted and her bowels disturbed' (Lam 1:20) by her weeping, that
'she sits among the nations and does not find rest, neither is there one
to console her.' (Lam 1:3,2) She has sought from the fathers of the
East[34] 'one who might share in her sorrow, and there was none, and
one to console her, and she did not find him, while she took gall for
her food and in her thirst drank vinegar' (cf Ps 68:21f), imitating the
sufferings of her spouse and Lord, 'who suffered for her that she might
follow his footsteps.' (cf I Pet 2:21)

69 Intercede, you patriarchs, from whose lineage she who now labours
on the earth was born; pray, you holy prophets, who see afflicted the
one of whom you formerly sang in prophetic utterance; be her
supporters, you apostles, you who ran to and fro across the whole
world like swift horses so that you might bring her together as the Lord
ascended over you. Especially you, blessed Peter, why do you not speak
on behalf of the sheep and lambs entrusted to you by the Lord of all,
in his great care and concern?[35] You, holy Paul, teacher of the
gentiles, who preached the gospel of God 'from Jerusalem as far as
Illyricum' (Rom 15:19), recognize what the Arian Vandals are doing,
and your captive sons who groan in lamentation; and all you holy
apostles, groan for us in unison!

70 But we know that we are unworthy of your prayers, because these
torments which have taken place to test us were the deserts, not of the
holy, but of those who deserved ill. But pray now for your evil sons,
because Christ, too, prayed, even for his enemies the Jews. May these
things which have been justly imposed on us suffice for our correction,
and may mercy for the wrongdoers be asked for at this very moment;
may the 'persecuting angel' be told '"Enough, now stay your hand."' (II
Sam 24:16) Who can fail to understand that our sinful and shameful
acts brought these things upon us, wandering away as we did from the
commandments of God and 'not wishing to walk in his law' (Ps 77:10)?

---

[34] Reading 'patribus' (with Halm), against 'partibus' (so Petschenig).

[35] One would have thought the 'cautela et sollicitudo' more likely to have been attributed
to Peter than the Lord, but the latter is meant here.

But, prostrate, we ask, through the one who moved you forward from being humble fishermen to your exalted position as apostles, that you do not spurn your wretched sinners.

[71 The most wicked Huniric held dominion in his kingdom for seven years and ten months. His death was in accordance with his merits, for as he rotted and the worms multiplied it seemed not so much a body as parts of his body which were buried. In addition, that transgressor of the revealed law who formerly came to them from the heresy of the Donatists, Nicasius, soon perished with a similar death.[36]]

---

[36] Nicasius is otherwise unknown. Courtois conjectures 'sic arius', or 'ut arius,' in place of the name (1954:16 n. 38), but I would be happy to accept it. Nevertheless, Courtois is almost certainly correct in regarding this passage as an interpolation (1954:16), together with Halm and Petschenig. The question is not advanced by Roncoroni 1977.

ABBREVIATIONS

CCSL	*Corpus Christianorum Series Latina*
CIL	*Corpus Inscriptionum Latinarum*
CSEL	*Corpus Scriptorum Ecclesiasticorum Latinorum*
MGH AA	*Monumenta Germaniae Historica Auctores Antiquissimi*
PG	*Patrologia Graeca*
PL	*Patrologia Latina*
PLRE	*Prosopography of the Later Roman Empire* vol. 2 (ed. J. Martindale)
PLS	*Patrologia Latina Supplementum*
SC	*Sources Chrétiennes*
TLL	*Thesaurus Linguae Latinae*

SELECT BIBLIOGRAPHY

EDITIONS

C. Halm *MGH AA* 2 1879

M. Petschenig *CSEL* 7 1881

PRIMARY SOURCES

Ambrose of Milan *De fide CSEL* 78

Augustine of Hippo *De civitate dei CCSL* 47f (trans. H. Bettenson, Harmondsworth 1972)

____   *Confessiones* ed. M. Skutella, Paris 1962 (trans. H. Chadwick, Oxford, 1991)

____   *Epistulae CSEL* 34, 44, 57f (trans. W. Parsons, Washington D. C. 1951 +)

____   *Retractationes CSEL* 36 (trans. M. E. Brogan, Washington D. C. 1968)

____   *Sermones PL* 38f

R. C. Blockley ed. and trans. *The fragmentary classicizing historians of the later Roman empire* Liverpool 1983

Cassiodorus *Variae MGH AA* 12 (condensed trans. Th. Hodgkin, London 1886)

Codex justinianus ed. P. Krüger, Berlin 1877

Codex theodosianus ed. Th. Mommsen and P. M. Meyer, Berlin 1905 (trans. C. Pharr, Princeton 1952)

Cyprian of Carthage *Epistulae* *CSEL* 3 (trans. G. W. Clarke, New York 1984 +)

Diadochus of Photike *Œuvres spirituelles* *SC* 5 bis

Ennodius *Vita Epifani* *MGH AA* 7 (trans G. M. Cook, in R. J. Deferrari ed. *Early Christian biographies* Washington D.C. 1952)

Evagrius *A History of the church* trans. E. Walford, London 1851

Expositio totius mundi et gentium *SC* 124

O. Fiebiger and L. Schmidt *Inschriftensammlung zur Geschichte der Ostgermanen* Vienna 1917 +

Gennadius *Liber de viris inlustribus* ed. E. C. Richardson, Leipzig 1896

Gregory of Rome *Dialogi* *SC* 151, 260, 265 (trans. O. J. Zimmermann, New York 1959)

Gregory of Tours *Libri historiarum* *MGH* *Scriptores rerum Merovingicarum* 1 (trans. *History of the Franks* O. M. Dalton, Oxford 1927)

Hydatius *Continuatio chronicorum* *MGH AA* 11

Isidore of Seville *Historia Gothorum Wandalorum Sueborum* *MGH AA* 11 (trans. G. Donini and G. B. Ford, Leiden 1970)

Jordanes *Getica MGH AA* 5 (trans. C. C. Mierow, Princeton 1908)

Laterculus regum VVandalorum et Alanorum *MGH AA* 13

Luxorius ed. and trans. M. Rosenblum, New York 1961

Marcellinus comes *Chronicon MGH AA* 11

Nestorius *The bazaar of Heracleides* trans. G. R. Driver and L. Hodgson, Oxford 1925

Optatus *Libri VII CSEL* 26

Possidius *Vita Augustini PL* 32:33ff (trans. M. M. Muller and R. J. Deferrari, in R. J. Deferrari ed. *Early Christian biographies* Washington D.C. 1952)

Procopius ed. and trans. H.B. Dewing, London 1914-1940

Prosper Tiro *Epitoma chronicon MGH AA* 9

Prudentius *Liber peristephanon PL* 60:277ff (trans. P. Clement Eagan, Washington D.C. 1962)

Quodvultdeus *Liber promissionum SC* 101f

Salvian *De gubernatione dei CSEL* 7 (trans. J.F. O'Sullivan, New York 1947)

De tempore barbarico PLS 3:287-298

Tertullian *Apologeticum CCSL* 1

Victor of Tunnunna *Chronica MGH AA* 11

Vigilius of Thapsus *Contra Varimadum PL* 62:351ff

Vita S. Danielis stylitae ed. H. Delehaye, *Les Saints stylites,* Brussels 1923 (trans. E. Davies and N. H. Baynes, *Three Byzantine saints*, Oxford 1948)

Zacharias *The Syriac chronicle known as that of Zachariah of Mytilene* trans. F.J. Hamilton and E.W. Brooks, London 1899

MODERN WORKS

L. Alfonsi 'L' «Historia persecutionis Africanae provinciae», ovvero il rifiuto di un ippocrita rinunciatarismo velleitario: "Romani" e "barbari"' *Siculorum gymnasium* 29 1976 1-18

O. W. Bairam-Ben and L. Ennalbi 'Note sur la topographie chrétienne de Carthage: Les mosaïques du monastère de Bigna' *Revue des études augustiniennes* 18 1982 3-18

C. Béla 'Geiserich és Vandáljai Rómában (455. Jún. 2-16)' *Acta antiqua et archaeologica* Suppl. 2 (Szeged, 1979), 25-32 (with summary in German)

S. A. Belyaev 'Ob odnom 'protivorechii' 'Istorii' Viktora iz Vity' in *Antichnost' i Sovremennost'* (Fest. F.A. Petrovskii) Moscow 1972 193f

F. Bertini *Autori latini in Africa sotto la dominazione vandalica* Genoa 1974

P. Brown *Augustine of Hippo* London 1967

R. Browning *Justinian and Theodora* London 1971

S. Calderone 'Circumcelliones' *La Parola del passato* 22 1967 94-109

A. Cameron 'Byzantine Africa - the literary evidence' in J.H. Humphrey ed. *Excavations at Carthage 1978 conducted by the University of Michigan VII* Ann Arbor 1982 pp. 29-62

G. Capello 'Il Latino di Vittore di Vita' *Atti della Società italiana per il progresso delle scienze (XXV riunione)* 16 1937 74-108

A. Carandini 'Pottery and the African Economy' in P. Garnsey, K. Hopkins and C. R. Whittaker ed. *Trade in the ancient economy* Berkeley 1983 pp.145-62

A. Chastagnol 'Les Gouverneurs de Byzacène et de Tripolitaine' *Antiquités africaines* 1 1967 119-34

F. Chatillon 'L'Afrique oubliée de Christian Courtois et les '*ignotae regiones*' de la *Vita Fulgentii*' *Revue du moyen âge latin* 11 1955 371-88

D. Claude 'Millenarius und thiuphadus' *Zeitschrift der Savigny-Stiftung für Rechtsgeschichte* Germanische Abt. 88 1971 181-90

F. M. Clover 'Carthage and the Vandals' *Excavations at Carthage* 7 1982a 1-22

―――― 'Emperor Worship in Vandal Africa' in *Romanitas -Christianitas* Berlin 1982b pp. 663-74

―――― 'Felix Karthago' *Dumbarton Oaks Papers* 40 1986 1-16

S. Costanza 'Considerazioni storiografice nell' Historia persecutionis Africanae provinciae di Vittore di Vita' *Bollettino di studi Latini* 6 1976 30-36

―――― 'Vittore di Vita e la *Historia persecutionis Africanae provinciae*' *Vetera Christianorum* 17 1980 230-268

―――― *Vittore di Vita: Storia della persecutione vandalica in Africa* Rome 1981

―――― '«Barbarus furor» in Vittore di Vita' in *Sodalitas Scritti in onore di Antonio Guarino* 2 Naples 1984 711-19

P. Courcelle *Histoire littéraire des grandes invasions germaniques* 3rd edn Paris 1964

C. Courtois *Victor de Vita et son oeuvre* Algiers 1954

―――― *Les Vandals et l'Afrique* Paris 1955

J. Cuoq *L'Église d'Afrique du nord du IIe au XIIe siècle* Paris 1984

F. Decret and M. Fantar *L'Afrique du nord dans l'antiquité* Paris 1981

H. Delehaye *Sanctus* Brussels 1927

J. Desanges 'Un témoignage peu connu de Procope sur la Numide vandale et byzantine' *Byzantion* 33 1963 41-69

H.-J. Diesner 'Sklaven und Verbannte, Märtyrer und Confessoren bei Victor Vitensis' *Philologus* 106 1962 101-120

_____ *Kirche und Staat im Spätrömischen Reich* Berlin 1964

_____ *Das Vandalenreich* Stuttgart 1966

_____ 'Prologomena zu einer Prosopogaphie des Vandalenreiches' *Jahrbuch der Österreichischen byzantinischen Gesellschaft* 17 1968 1-15

_____ 'Zum vandalischen Post- und Verkehrswesen' *Philologus* 112 1968 283-87

_____ 'Grenzen und Grenzverteidigung des Vandalenreiches' in *Studi in onore di Edoardo Volterra* 3 Milan 1971 pp. 481-90

G. G. Diligenskii *Severnaya Afrika v IV-V vekakh* Moscow 1961

Y. Duval *Loca sanctorum: Le culte des martyres en Afrique du IVe au VIIe siècle* Rome 1982

L. Ennalbi *Les inscriptions funéraires chrétiennes de la basilique de Sainte-Monique à Carthage* Rome 1975

F. Ferrère 'Langue et style de Victor de Vita' *Revue de philologie* 25 1901 320-36

J. D. Frage ed. *The Cambridge History of Africa* 2 Cambridge 1978

W. H. C. Frend *The Donatist church* 2nd impression Oxford 1971

———   'The early Christian church in Carthage' *Excavations at Carthage* 3 1977 21-40

———   'Donatist and catholic: The organisation of Christian communities in the north African countryside' in *Cristianizzazione ed organizzazione ecclesiastica delle campagne nell' alto medioevo: Espansione e resistenze* Spoleto 1982 (=Settimane di studio del Centro italiano di studi sull' alto medioevo 28) 601-634

E.-F. Gautier *Genséric roi des vandales* Paris 1932

A. Giardina ed. *Società romana e impero tardoantico* 3 *Le merci gli insediamenti* Rome 1986

W. Goffart *Barbarians and Romans, A.D. 418-584: The techniques of accommodation* Princeton 1980

R. Heuberger 'Vandalische Reichskanzlei und Königsurkunden im Vergleich mit verwandten Einrichtungen und Erscheinungen' *Mitteilungen des Österreichischen Instituts für Geschichtsforschung* Ergänzband 11 1929

R. Hodges and D. Whitehouse *Mohammed Charlemagne and the origins of Europe* London 1983

T. Hodgkin *Italy and her invaders* 2nd edn vol. 2 book 3 Oxford 1892

H. R. Hurst and S.P. Roskams *Excavations at Carthage: The British mission* vol. 1/1 Sheffield 1984

A. H. M. Jones *The later Roman empire 284-602* Oxford 1964

G. G. Koenig 'Wandalische Grabfunde des 5. und 6. Jhs' *Madrider Mitteilungen* 22 1981 299-360

A.-M. La Bonnadière *Recherches de chronologie augustinienne* Paris 1965

H. Leclercq *L'Afrique chrétienne* 2 Paris 1904a

──── *Les martyrs* 3 Paris 1904b

B. Löfstedt 'Drei patristische Beiträge' *Arctos* 16 1982 65-72

J.-L. Maier *L'Episcopat de l'Afrique romaine, vandale et byzantine* Rome 1973

A. Mandouze *Prosopographie chrétienne du bas-empire* 1 *Prosopographie de l'Afrique chrétienne (303-533)* Paris 1982

R. A. Markus 'Christianity and dissent in Roman north Africa: Changing perspectives in recent work' *Studies in church history* 9 1972 21-36

H.-I. Marrou 'Diadoque de Photiké et Victor de Vita' *Revue des études anciennes* 44 1943 225-232

──── 'Le valeur historique de Victor de Vita' *Les cahiers de Tunisie* 15 1967 205-208

J. Martindale *The Prosopography of the later Roman empire* 2 Cambridge 1980

F. Martroye *Genséric* Paris 1907

F. Miltner 'Vandalen' Pauly-Wissowa ed. *Realencyclopädie der classischen Altertumswissenschaft* 8 298-335

G. Mokhtar ed. *General History of Africa* 2 *Ancient Civilizations of Africa* Paris 1981

J. Orlandis *Historia de España 4 Época Visigoda (409-711)* Madrid 1987

M. Overbeck *Untersuchungen zum Afrikanischen Senatsadel in der Spätantike* Kallmünz Opf. 1973

A. Pastorino 'Osservazione sulla *Historia persecutionis Africanae provinciae* di Vittore di Vita' in S. Calderone ed. *La storiografia ecclesiastica nella tarda antichità* Messina 1980

M. Petschenig 'Die handschriftliche Ueberlieferung des Victor von Vita' *Sitzungsberichte der Philosophisch- Historische Classe der Kaiserlichen Akademie der Wissenschaften* Vienna 96 1880

R. Pitkäranta 'Stilistischer Kommentar zur "Passio septem martyrum"' *Arctos* 8 1974 127-37

_____ *Studien zum Latein des Victor Vitensis* Helsinki 1978

D. Pringle *The defence of Byzantine Africa from Justinian to the Arab conquest* Oxford 1981

P. Riché *Education and culture in the barbarian West* trans. J. J. Contreni Columbia 1976

D. Romano 'Osservazioni sul prologo alla Historia di Vittore Vitense' *Atti della Accademia di scienze lettere e arti di Palermo* 4th ser. 20 1962 19-36

A. Roncoroni 'Sulla morte di re Unerico' *Romanobarbarica* 2 1977 247-57

_____ 'Vittore Vitense, *Historia persecutionis Africanae provinciae*, III, 55-60' *Siculorum gymnasium* 29 1979 387-95

V. Saxer *Morts martyrs reliques en Afrique chrétienne aux premiers siècles* Paris 1980

M. Schanz *Geschichte der Römischen Literatur* 4 Munich 1904

L. Schmidt *Geschichte der Wandalen* 2nd edn Munich 1942

P. Senay and M. Beauregard 'L'*Aedes Memoriae*: Un témoignage antique sur le monument circulaire de Carthage' *Cahiers des études anciennes* 19 1986 78-85

E. Stein *Histoire du bas-empire* 1 Paris 1959

Y. Thébert 'L'Évolution urbaine dans les provinces orientales de l'Afrique romaine tardive' *Opus* 1983 99-131

C. R. Whittaker 'Land and labour in North Africa' *Klio* 60 1978 1-62

H. Wolfram 'Gotisches Königtum und römisches Kaisertum von Theodosius dem Grossen bis Justinian I.' *Frühmittelatlerlichen Studien* 13 1979 1-28

_____ *Intitulatio* Graz 1967

P. Wynn 'Rufinus of Aquilea's *Ecclesiastical history* and Victor of Vita's *History of the Vandal persecution*' *Classica et mediaevalia* 41 1990 187-98

INDEX